# MILITARY AVIATION REVIEW

WW I and WW 2

Flying Headgear
Flying Clothing
Uniforms
Life Jackets / Parachutes
Escape / Evasion / Survival
Wings / Badges / Insignia
Aircraft Parts / Relics
Aviation Ephemera

WWW.TRENDINGCOLLECTIBLES.COM

INTRODUCTION
BY
MICK J. PRODGER

Elm Grove Publishing

ISBN 978-1-943492-00-8

Trending Collectibles
is an imprint of
ELM GROVE PUBLISHING
San Antonio, Texas, USA
WWW.ELMGROVEPUBLISHING.COM

Book design by
designpanache

Also available as an e-book

# CONTENTS

# KEY TO NATIONAL EMBLEMS

For quick identification, national emblems of the country / air force of origin are used. Flying clothing, equipment and even uniforms made in one country were sometimes issued to personnel in other country's air forces, so, in a few cases, multiple national emblems are used.

Readers may notice that there is a heavy preponderance of Second World War British flying clothing and equipment. This is because it was used not only by aircrews of the RAF and Fleet Air Arm, but also by the Allies, including the United States, British Commonwealth countries, Europeans who escaped before the German occupation and formed units attached to the RAF, the Soviet Union, and even the Italian Air Force after 1943. Most collections of Allied aviation items will contain a high proportion of British flying equipment.

 USA (Army Air Service, Air Corps, AAF and USN)

 UK and British Commonwealth (RFC, RAF, RCAF, RAAF, RNZAF, SAAF and Fleet Air Arm)

 France (Free French)

 Germany (Luftwaffe)

 USSR

 Italy (Regia Aeronautica)

 Japan (Army and Navy Air Forces)

 Czechoslovakia

All sale prices are listed in US dollars ($), British pounds sterling (£) and Euros (€). International currency exchange rates fluctuate daily and all exchange rates were calculated at the time the information was gathered. All currency conversions must therefore be regarded as approximate.

While every effort has been made to report the sales of these items accurately, the publisher cannot accept any liability for errors, nor for the loss, financial or otherwise, incurred by reliance placed on the information contained in this publication.

Prices quoted in this book are market prices; that is to say the actual price a collector has paid to a professional dealer. If you have a single piece or a collection to sell, please bear in mind that professional sellers do this for a living. Do not expect to receive full market price from dealers; you will be treated fairly and honestly and will receive the best possible price, because they have contact with collectors who will pay the fair market price. It is hard work and profits are often modest. Reputable dealers spend many years earning their credentials, stand behind their product, guarantee authenticity and are the best people with whom to buy, sell or trade.

# INTRODUCTION

I have never cared much for the idea of "price guides". Opinions of what something should, could or might be worth are of little value to collectors in the "here and now".

On the other hand, a Market Report – regularly updated and based on actual sale prices of real items – is a very helpful tool for collectors, professional sellers, museum underwriters and anyone with an interest in the preservation of military and historical artifacts.

This Market Report features recent sales of aviation collectibles based on information gathered from internationally known, well-respected, reputable dealers and private collectors. It includes common and not-so-common items, each with a photograph and brief description. It is designed for quick and easy reference for both collectors and sellers, and intended to help establish fair market values as well as an understanding of how those values change over time. While no resource of this type could possibly include an example of every single item of interest to collectors, this handy reference includes a very comprehensive range of collectibles so that buyers and sellers alike will be able to gain a useful impression.

I hope it will be of value to old and seasoned collectors, and that it will also encourage new collectors who may be confused by the array of artifacts and vast range of prices, especially found in online auctions. For anyone new to the hobby, the world of collecting can be very intimidating!

There will always be car boot sales, flea markets and estate sales, as well as social networking sites and online auctions, where knowldgeable collectors will be able to snag a bargain once in a while – and long may those opportunities continue! This work is not intended to "spoil the fun", but to provide a reliable go-to resource of actual market prices, so that over time, collectors will be able to gain a better sense of value of their collections.

Mick J. Prodger

# FOREWORD

Collecting has always been for fun, but as the popularity of vintage militaria increases, so does its market value. These days, many financial advisors encourage people to include a percentage of collectibles in their investment / retirement portfolio – but a wise investment requires knowledge based on real sales trends, not just opinions, and that kind of information can be difficult to come by – even with the advanced resources of the internet – unless the investor is willing to spend a lot of time researching. TRENDING COLLECTIBLES MILITARY AVIATION REVIEW has done the hard work, gathering and filtering accurate sales information from universally recognized and respected professionals, as well as knowledgeable private collectors.

Establishing real values based on actual collecting trends will not only help collectors and sellers to gain valuable insight into the collecting marketplace, it may also help in establishing values for insurance purposes, and the recognition of aviation artifacts as a worthwhile area of collecting for investment purposes.

Interest in all things antique, vintage and collectible is constantly increasing, with more and more collectors tending to specialize in specific fields. TRENDING COLLECTIBLES MILITARY AVIATION REVIEW 2015 is the first edition of what is to become an annual review of current market values in the rapidly growing and highly specialized field of aviation artifacts.

In addition to the annual Market Reports, there is an online members' blog where collectors can compare notes, share information from their own buying and selling experiences, and receive quarterly updates on current collecting trends.

For more information, visit

**WWW.TRENDINGCOLLECTIBLES.COM**

---

TRENDING COLLECTIBLES MILITARY AVIATION REVIEW offers comprehensive information on recent sales of aviation collectibles ranging from flying helmets, jackets and wings to parachutes, escape kits and souvenir items, with prices ranging from a few dollars (or pounds) to five figures. It is not intended, nor would it be possible, to list examples of every aviation artifact sought by collectors, but to provide a good selection and wide range of sale prices so that, year by year, collectors can follow the trends of the collecting marketplace.

# ACKNOWLEDGEMENTS

I have been collecting aviation items for almost 30 years, and in that time it has been both a pleasure and a privilege to meet and become firm friends with many knowledgeable individuals. People who have always been willing to share their knowledge, experience and wisdom with me.

In preparing this inaugural work for TRENDING COLLECTIBLES, I contacted several well-respected dealers who specialize in aviation artifacts, as well as a number of advanced collectors, and asked them if they would be willing to share actual sales information. I also asked them for advice, guidance, thoughts and opinions on the basic concept and how best to catalogue the artifacts. The responses I received were universally encouraging. It would seem the aviation collecting world is definitely ready for this kind of Market Report.

Thank you to all my good friends and professionals who have helped me to gather this information together, especially Ron Burkey, David Farnsworth, Simon Lannoy, Geoff Pringle and Neil Seaton. Thanks also John Conway, Jon Maguire and Tod Rathbone for their help, friendship and encouragement with this project.

Last but not least, thank you to the many collectors who have contributed information to this project and whose privacy I respect far too much to name. You know who you are!

All of these people gave generously of their time and have received no compensation from myself or the publisher and none of the items catalogued are identified either to the seller or the buyer. That said I am happy to recommend the following websites as reliable and trusted resources for anyone looking to begin, or add to, a collection of aviation memorabilia.

www.flyingtigerantiques.com

www.historicflyingclothing.com

www.oldnautibits.com

www.themilitarydealers.com

www.vintageflyinghelmets.com

# FLYING HEADGEAR

Flying helmets
Goggles
Sunglasses
Oxygen masks
Radio and communications gear
Accessories

WW I – early 1920s leather flying helmet with goggles. Standard Army Air Service issue with flaps over each ear and a snap to secure the goggle strap.
**SOLD for**
**$235 / £160 / €220**

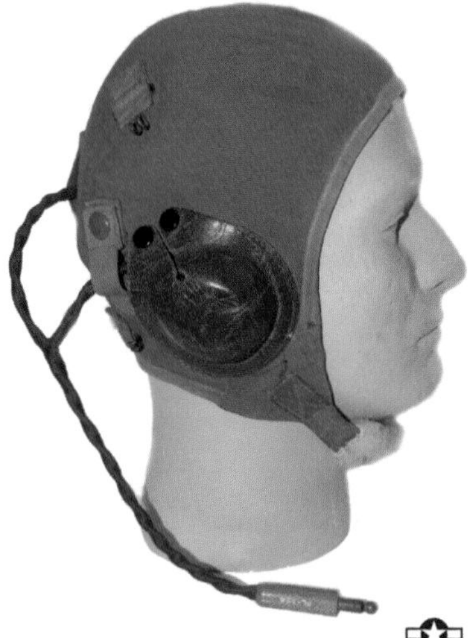

WW II USAAF Type A-9 flying helmet in excellent condition, fitted with leather ear cups and R-14 receivers with braided cord and plug.
**SOLD for**
**$138 / £90 / €122**

WW II USAAF Type A-11 intermediate flying helmet. Second type with 4 snaps each side. Shows light use, no abuse or damage, good decal, complete with ANB-H-1 receivers, cord and plug.
**SOLD for**
**$250 / £163 / €220**

WW II USAAF Type A-11 intermediate flying helmet. First type with 3 snaps each side. Medium size, made by Selby Shoe Company. Shows normal use. Good condition.
**SOLD for**
**$113 / £75 / €104**

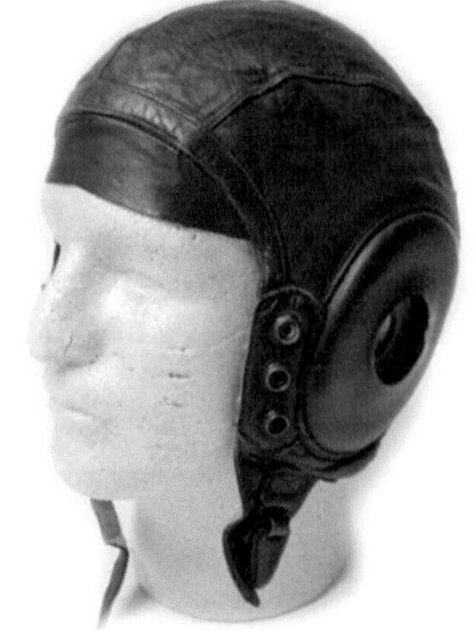

WW II Army Air Forces Type A-11 flying helmet by Swan Shoe Co. Size Medium. Excellent condition, inside and out, probably unissued.
SOLD for
$248 / £165 / €229

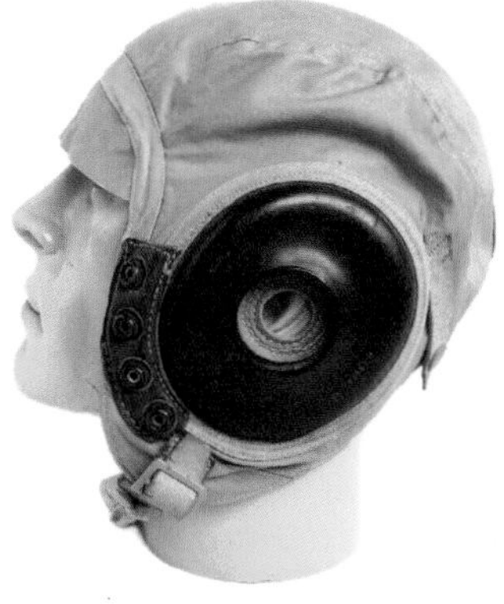

WW II Army Air Forces Type AN-H-15 flying helmet by Bates Shoe Co. Size large. Chin strap has some surface cracking but retains the velvet chin pad. The inside of the helmet is clean but the chamois ear pads are soiled. Nice clear label.
SOLD for
$77 / £50 / €68

WW II AAF M-3 Anti-flak helmet. Essentially a modified M1 steel helmet with an adjustable webbing suspension liner and cut away sides with hinged ear flaps. Overall very good condition with some surface corrosion.
SOLD for
$348 / £235 / €328

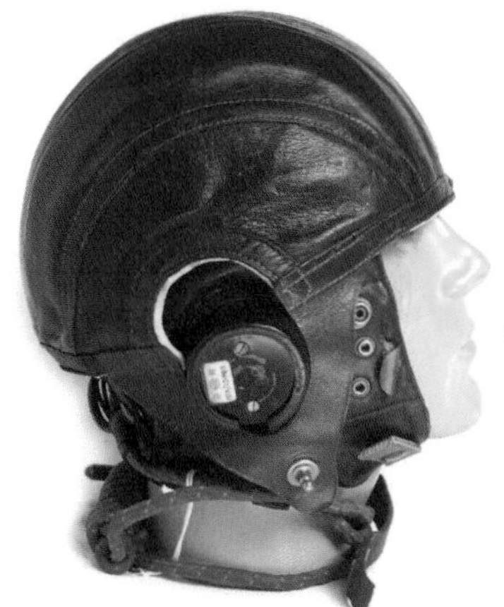

WWII AAF M-4 Anti-flak helmet (also known as the "Grow" helmet after its designer, Colonel Malcolm Grow, 8th Air Force Chief Flight Surgeon). Manufactured in England by Wilkinson Sword and issued to both AAF and RAF crews. Excellent condition, with some storage wear.
SOLD for
$1880 / £1250 / €1734

WW II AAF M-5 Anti-flak helmet with unknown marking on one hinged ear piece " '73 Rules". Differs from the M-3 in having elongated ear covers. Showing average use and missing chin strap, but overall good condition.
**SOLD for**
**$200 / £130 / €175**

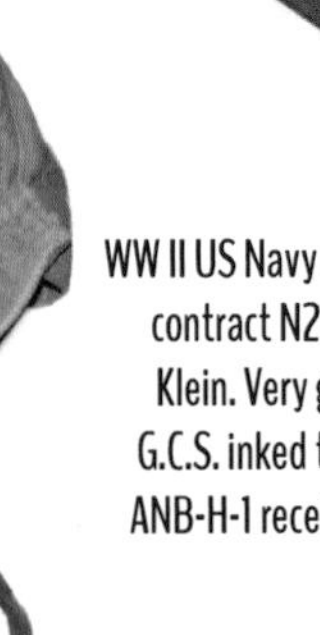

WW II US Navy summer flying helmet, contract N288s-27405 by Slote & Klein. Very good condition, initials G.C.S. inked to brow and fitted with ANB-H-1 receivers with braided cord and plug.
**SOLD for**
**$82 / £53 / €73**

Pre-WW II Army Air Corps Type B-6 flying goggles. Separate rubber cushions in good shape, nickel plated frames with distinctive"wings" emblem to centre and dark tinted "sky lookout" lenses.
**SOLD for**
**$350 / £228 / €308**

A very good pair of "Skyway" goggles, used extensively during WW II, not only by aircrews, but also by tank crews and Motor-cyclists. Overall condition is very good, the goggles perhaps never having been used.
**SOLD for**
**$184 / £120 / €165**

WW II AAF Type AN-6530 F flying goggles with the tube-type vents on either side. Clear lenses and one-piece rubber cushion. Used by the Army and Navy during WW II.
SOLD for
$250 / £170 / €235

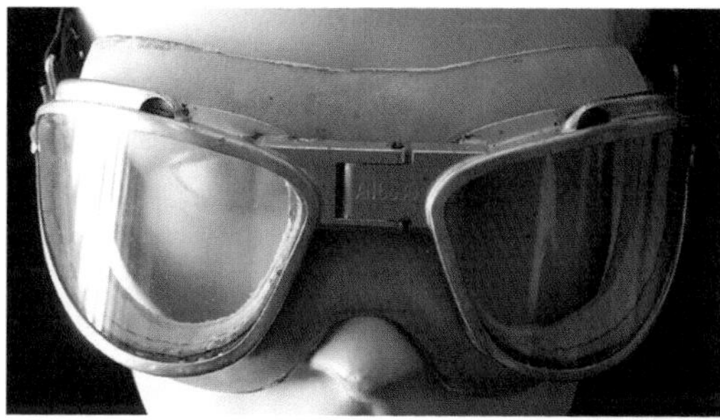

A similar pair of WW II Army Air Forces Type AN-6530 Pilot goggles with Chas. Fischer Spring Co. maker's mark under left lens frame. This pair with the streamlined vents.
SOLD for
$320 / £218 / €300

WW II AAF replacement lenses for B-7 / AN-6530 Flying goggles by Bausch & Lomb Optical Co. Specification No. AN-DD-L-236. Clear glass lenses in original tissue wrapping and envelope.
SOLD for
$47 / £30 / €41

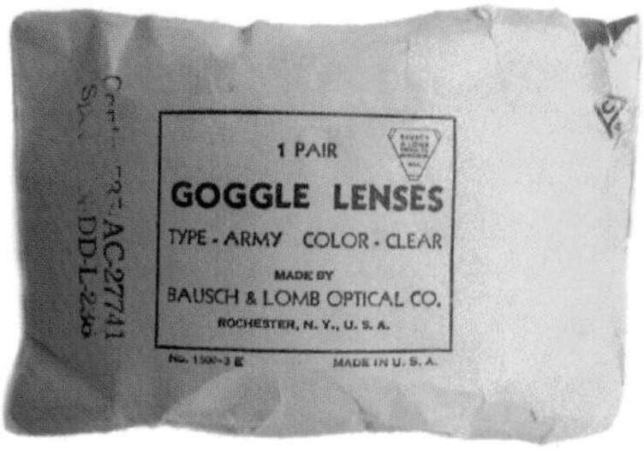

WW II AAF replacement lenses for B-7 / AN-6530 flying goggles by American Optical. Specification No. AN-DD-L-236. Green glass lenses in original tissue wrapping.
SOLD for
$54 / £35 / €47

Pre-WW II US Navy Mk I Pilot goggles by Willson. Clear glass lenses in gunmetal plated frames with one piece rubber cushion. In good condition.
**SOLD for**
**$375 / £244 / €330**

WW II US Navy M-1944 goggles by Polaroid, complete with red flip screen for observing tracer, and working mechanism. Goggles are 1945 dated with a clear lens. The flip screen appears to be made from another lens.
**SOLD for**
**$250 / £163 / €224**

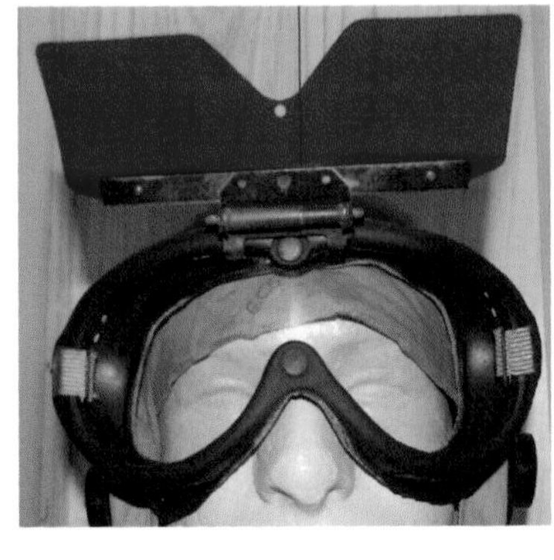

WW II AAF B-8 Flying goggles, complete with box and spare lenses. A very good pair in issue box, with 6 spare lenses and instruction booklet. All in very good condition and ideal for display.
**SOLD for**
**$120 / £80 / €110**

WW II AAF B-8 goggles kit with issue box, several extra lenses and instruction booklet, all in excellent condition.
**SOLD for**
**$120 / £80 / €110**

WW II AAF Type B-8 Flying goggles in good condition, complete with box of issue, one extra amber lens, extra lens storage pouches and instruction booklet.
SOLD for
$118 / £77 / €104

WW II Army Air Corps Type D-1 sunglasses. Light green tinted lenses, folding centre hinge marked USAC, wire folding arms lacking plastic covering.

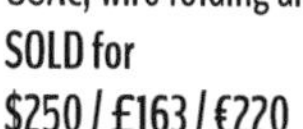

SOLD for
$250 / £163 / €220

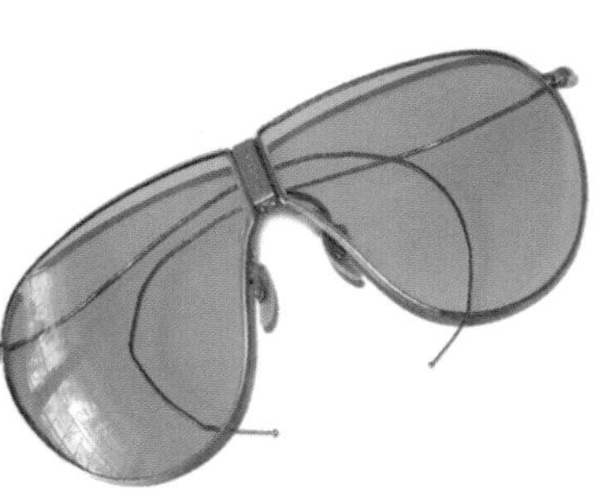

WW II AAF sunglasses. Scarce early aviator sunglasses with brown lenses by American Optical Company (A.O.) in leather issue case with a paper label.
SOLD for
$245 / £161 / €230

WW II AAF sunglasses by Bausch & Lomb in original leather case. Light green tinted lenses.
SOLD for
$185 / £124 / €176

WW II AAF Type A-8B oxygen mask in excellent condition including fully functional rebreather bag /bladder. Correct wartime cardboard stiffeners, Bakelite nose form plus leather strap with leather extension clip.
SOLD for
$550 / £365 / €512

WW II AAF Type A-9 oxygen mask. Excellent original mask dated 1.42 showing light use but no damage, retaining nosewire and straps as well as hose and connector. Moulded in light grey / green rubber and manufactured by Acushnet.
SOLD for
$610 / £397 / €535

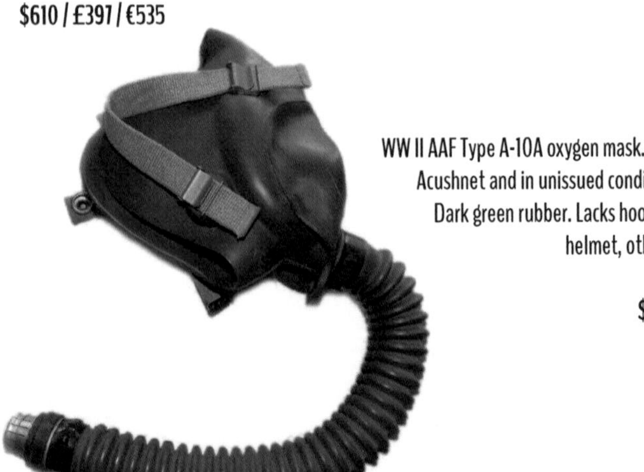

WW II AAF Type A-10A oxygen mask. Manufactured by Acushnet and in unissued condition, dated 4.44. Dark green rubber. Lacks hook for attaching to helmet, otherwise excellent.
SOLD for
$179 / £116 / €158

WW II AAF Type A-14 oxygen mask. A good complete example in its original 1944 dated storage box with instructions, headband modification harness and various accessories. Dated 10.44 the face mask, harness and oxygen tube are in generally good condition. The storage box is marked medium, though the mask itself is stamped Small. No microphone is present in the mask. Some crazing to the rubber section of the harness but overall is excellent. Box is in very good undamaged condition.
**SOLD for**
**$182 / £120 / €168**

WW II AAF Boxed Type A-14 oxygen mask. Dated 5-45. Size small. Label printed '8th A.F. Modification'. Some sections of the face-piece have hardened. Webbing and rubber parts of the harness are generally very good and hose is excellent. Original cellophane wrapping, spares envelope, general instruction leaflet and instruction sheet for 8th A.F. modification included.
**SOLD for**
**$210 / £135 / €188**

WW II AAF silk scarf made from approx. 30 x 12 inch section of parachute canopy, with the addition of silk fringes to both ends.
**SOLD for**
**$26 / £17 / €24**

Pre-WW II US Air Corps Type T-20 throat microphone. Leather covered microphone pick-ups.
**SOLD for**
**$75 / £50 / €70**

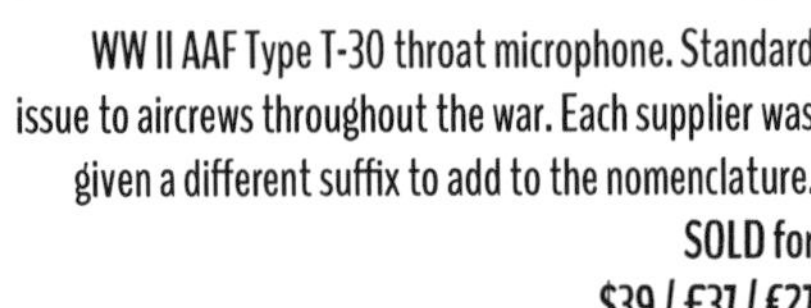

WW II AAF Type T-30 throat microphone. Standard issue to aircrews throughout the war. Each supplier was given a different suffix to add to the nomenclature.
**SOLD for**
**$39 / £31 / €27**

A similar WW II AAF Type T-30 throat microphone. This is a T-30S made by Universal Microphone Co. of Inglewood, California.
**SOLD for**
**$60 / £40 / €57**

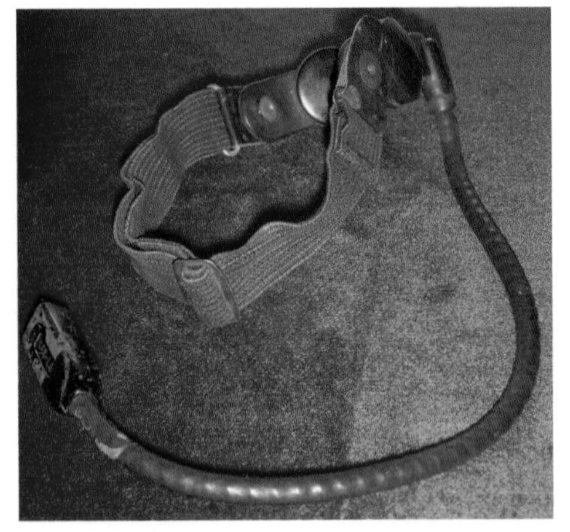

WW II AAF T-44A microphone and wiring loom (CO-287) by Western Electric Co. Inc. for use in RAF aircraft. Includes US made RAF style plug and AAF JK-26 socket.
**SOLD for**
**$189/ £125 / €176**

WW II AAF Type R-14 radio receivers. The type used in early flying helmets such as the A-9, B-5 and B-6. Also used in tanks and armoured vehicles.
SOLD for
$76 / £50/ €71

WW II AAF headset for most later flying helmets including A-11, AN-H-15, AN-H-16 etc. Comprises HS-38 loom with PL-354 plug and a matched pair of ANB-H-1 receivers by Shure Brothers of Chicago. Excellent, unused condition.
SOLD for
$189 / £125 / €176

WW II HB-7 aircrew headset as worn over the "50 mission crusher." With ANB-H-1 receivers by Utah, Chicago and red PL354 plug. Headset shows light use but MC-162A rubber cushions are in only far condition.
SOLD for
$83 / £55 / €78

WW II AAF headset for most later flying helmets including A-11, AN-H-15, AN-H-16 etc. Comprises HS-38 loom with PL-354 plug and a matched pair of ANB-H-1 receivers by Shure Brothers of Chicago. Excellent, unused condition.
SOLD for
$189 / £125 / €176

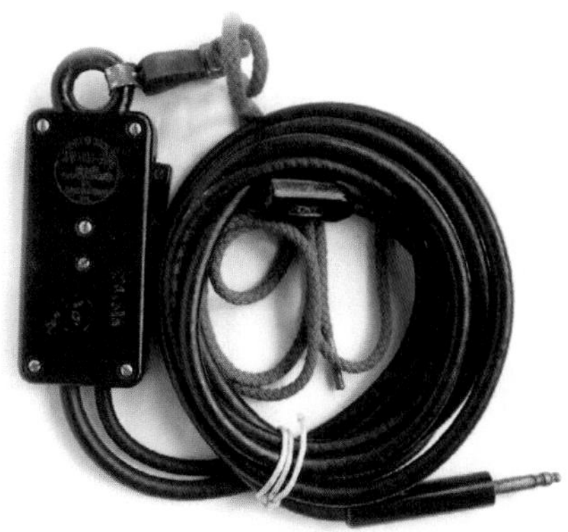

WW I RFC cowl flying helmet. Condition of the exterior of the helmet is very good, leather remains supple, retains its original colour and is without tears or scuffs. Chamois interior is excellent but fur lined section is in poor condition. War Department issued helmet, with two large WD stamps inside. A wonderful looking helmet that displays well.

**SOLD for**
**$1808 / £1200 / €1690**

A similar WW I issue RFC cowl flying helmet of a slightly different pattern but also marked with the WD War Department acceptance / issue stamp. This example manufactured without the trapezoid ear flaps but retaining the padded cylinders for wind deflection. Interior soiled and with damage to the fur lining.

**SOLD for**
**$995 / £661 / €930**

Pre-WW II private purchase flying helmet by Lewis of London. A popular style which was also offered in dark brown or black leather. White cotton with pockets to each side for installing Gosport receivers.

**SOLD for**
**$115 / £75 / €101**

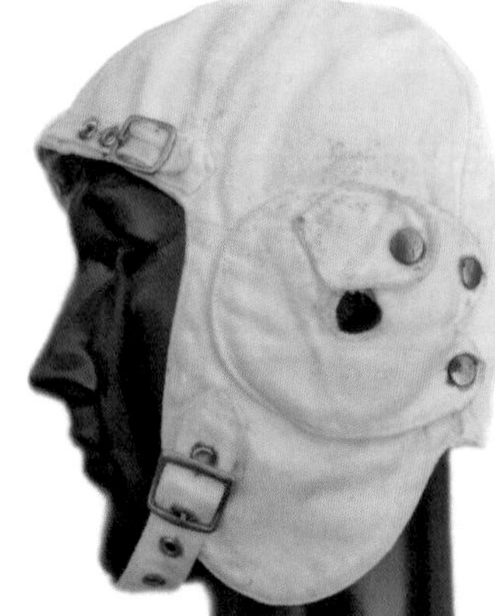

War Department flying or motorcycle helmet, circa 1940, with roll-up ear flaps and brow tightening strap associated with early flying helmets. Marked with the broad arrow. Examples of this helmet have been seen with various aircraft factory names printed on the chin strap.
**SOLD for**
**$131 / £85 / €115**

A similar War Department helmet. This example is clearly stamped, "Handley Page Aircraft Co. Property of Flight Test Unit" and carries a War Department stamp on the knitted wool lining. The helmet is in good condition although it is a little stiff.
**SOLD for**
**$144 / £95 / €134**

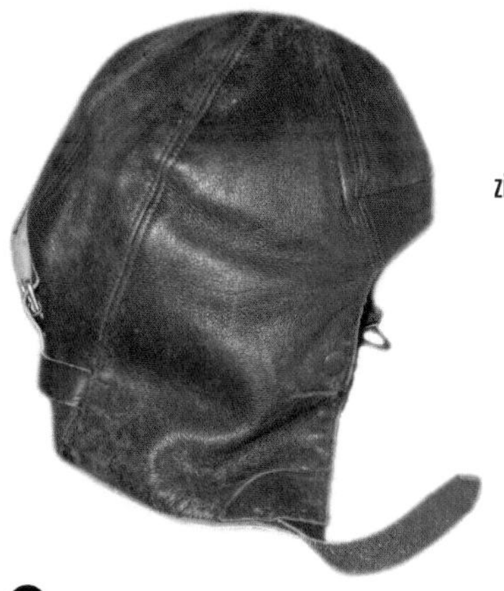

RAF Type B flying helmet as issued, without the zipped compartments for receivers. 1940 dated label manufactured by Waddingtons. Extra large (size 4).
**SOLD for**
**$325 / £215 / €303**

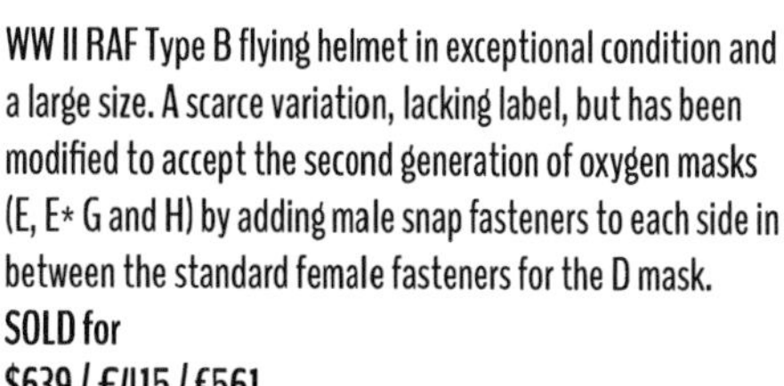

WW II RAF Type B flying helmet in exceptional condition and a large size. A scarce variation, lacking label, but has been modified to accept the second generation of oxygen masks (E, E* G and H) by adding male snap fasteners to each side in between the standard female fasteners for the D mask.
**SOLD for**
**$639 / £415 / €561**

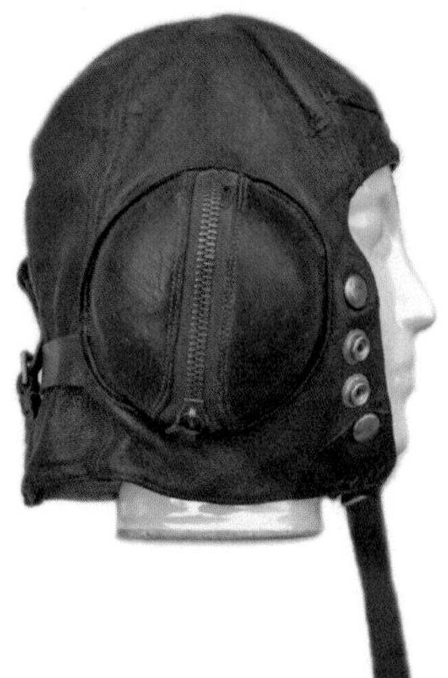

WW II RAF Type B flying helmet dated 1938. An outstanding example, size 2, by Frank Bryan and showing almost no signs of use. Both zips are perfect with leather pull tabs still in place. Inside, the chamois is clean, showing the remains of the Air Ministry stamp.

**SOLD for**
**\$716 / £475 / €666**

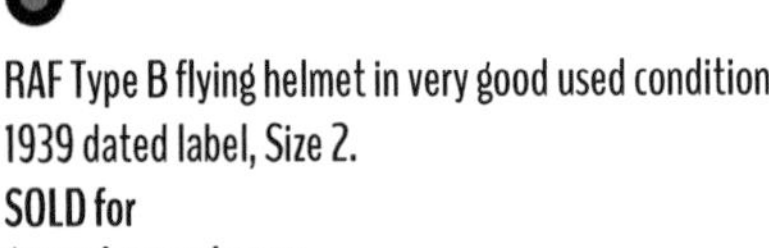

RAF Type B flying helmet in very good used condition. 1939 dated label, Size 2.

**SOLD for**
**\$650 / £422 / €570**

RAF Type B flying helmet with guide plates for the Mk IV series of goggles. The helmet has had whitewash applied overall in the past, now almost vanished from the leather, with the plates still showing remains. (Probably added for visibility in the event of a water landing). AM label showing a size 2.

**SOLD for**
**\$679 / £450 / €632**

WW II RAF Early pattern Type C flying helmet, stores ref. 22C/450. Size 2. (6-7/8 – 7). Leather is in excellent overall condition with only light use/wear.

**SOLD for**
**\$434 / £285 / €385**

WW II RAF second pattern, internally wired Type C flying helmet, stores ref. 22C/878. Size 2 (6-7/8 – 7). Fully wired with a mid tan coloured loom, matched 10A/13466 receivers and black cased bell jack plug.
SOLD for
$498 / £325 / €447

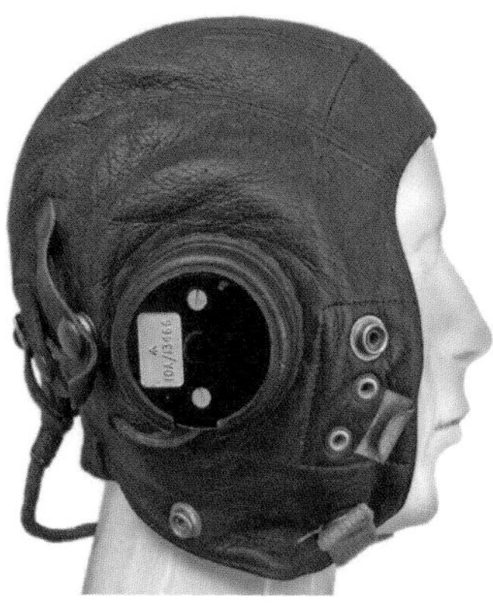

RAF Type C flying helmet, second type, second pattern, with internal wiring loom and 5 leather tabs to rear. Wired with receivers, cord and plug. Size 2.
SOLD for
$407 / £270 / €380

WW II RAF Type C flying helmet. Second pattern with receiver cups carefully removed and replaced with matching circles of brown leather, presumably for motoring / motorcycling use.
SOLD for
$110 / £72 / €101

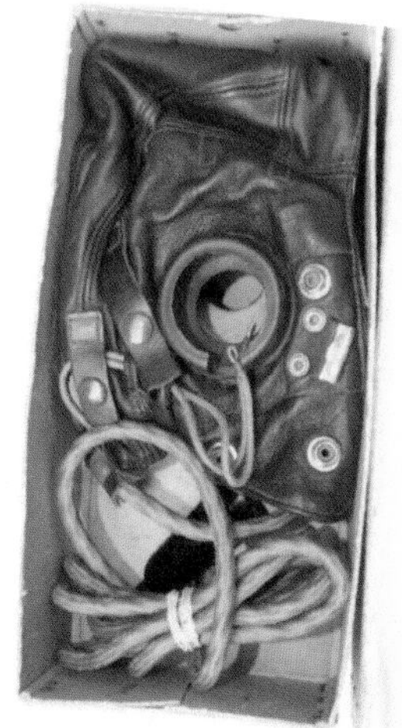

RAF Type C flying helmet still contained in its original storage / issue box. The Helmet is a size 2 in excellent unissued condition, without receivers but complete with wiring loom.
SOLD for
$221 / £150 / €212

RAF Type C* (C-star) helmet. The Type C* was essentially a wartime Type C with later NATO type wiring and plug for use in 1950s aircraft. Includes a post war Type H oxygen mask.
**SOLD for**
**$287 / £190 / €268**

RAF Type D flying helmet, first pattern with external wiring, together with a microphone carrier mask and Type 28 microphone assembly. All in good condition.
**SOLD for**
**$1500 / £995 / €1403**

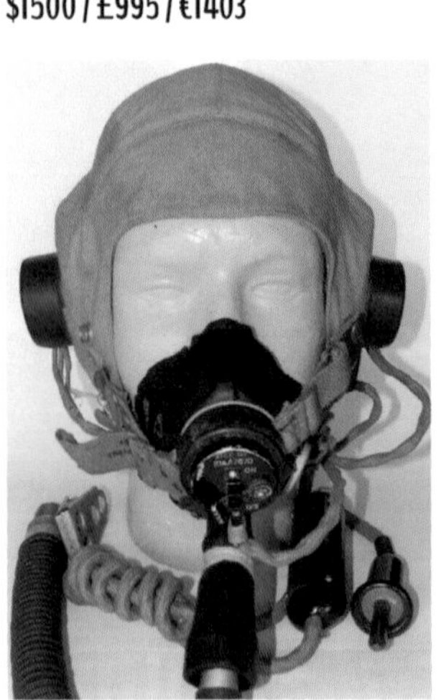

WW II RAF Type D helmet, Type E* (E-star) oxygen mask plus original photos, medal ribbons, sweetheart wings and papers, all named to a Desert Air Force pilot. Helmet is second pattern fitted with an early external loom and impedance switch box. Mask shows age but displays well.
**SOLD for**
**$975 / £647 / €912**

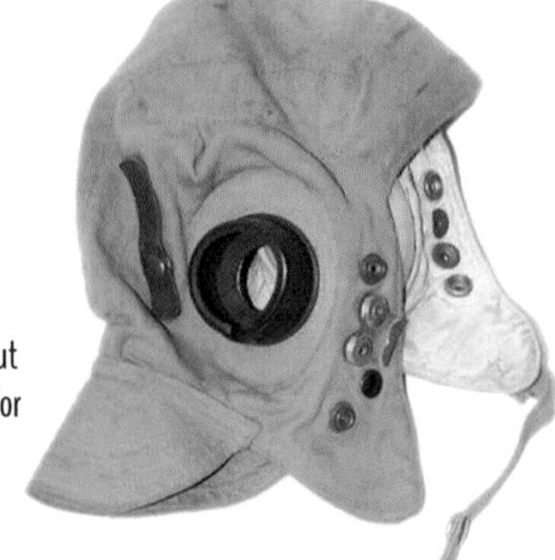

RAF Type D flying helmet, first pattern but without wiring or receivers fitted. Good condition except for a few marks from normal service use.
**SOLD for**
**$260 / £175 / €244**

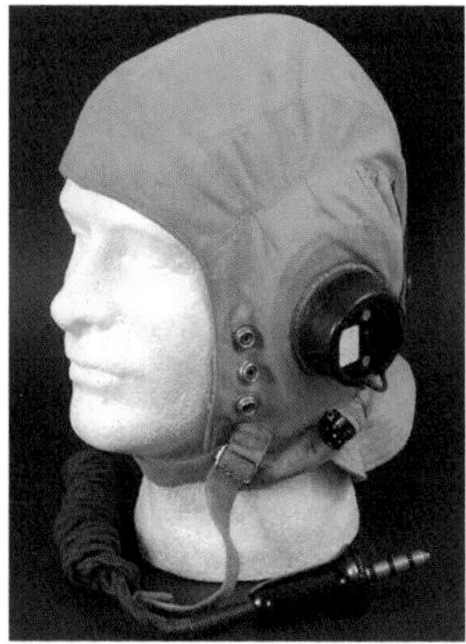

RAF Type D flying helmet, size 3 (large), fully wired with an internal loom and showing very little signs of use, the exterior being in virtually unissued condition.
SOLD for
$1500 / £330 / €1403

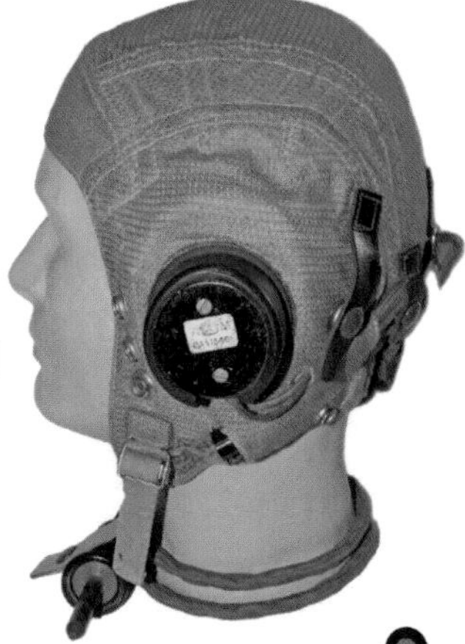

WW II RAF Type E flying helmet. Second pattern with internal wiring loom fitted, receivers and appropriate plugs. Size 2 in excellent condition.
SOLD for
$275 / £180/ €247

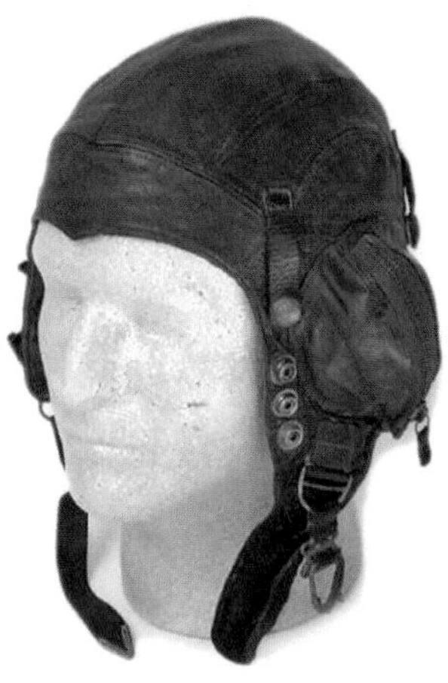

WW II Fleet Air Arm Type C helmet. Early, externally wired version. Appearance is quite good but with wear and use, and minor damage to the chamois lining. Leather chin cover shows the faint impression of the Admiralty crown and anchor.
SOLD for
$180 / £120 / €170

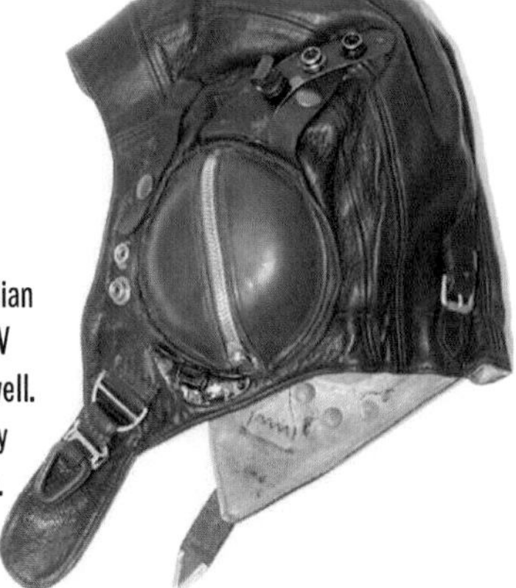

An unusual Fleet Air Arm Type C Helmet fitted with Canadian made zip ear compartments and guide plates for the Mk IV series of goggles. A rare size 4, the helmet displays very well. The only point of note is a small slit in the leather, slightly below the right lower plate. Chamois shows very light use.
SOLD for

$565 / £375 / €530

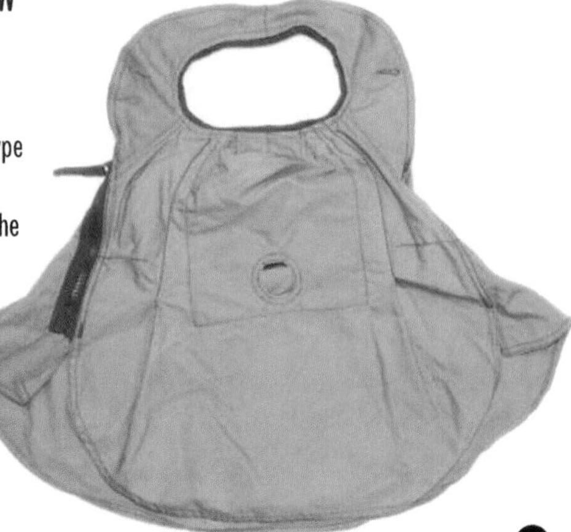

WW II RAF gunner's hood. Retains the strip for stitching to the neck of the C Type Helmet. Overall condition is excellent with the Dot zip working perfectly and the "Windak" label intact.
**SOLD for**
**$130 / £85 / €120**

RAAF flying helmet, similar to the RAF Type B. Dark brown leather with brow strap and zipped ear compartments. Dated 1942.
**SOLD for**
**$260 / £170 / €234**

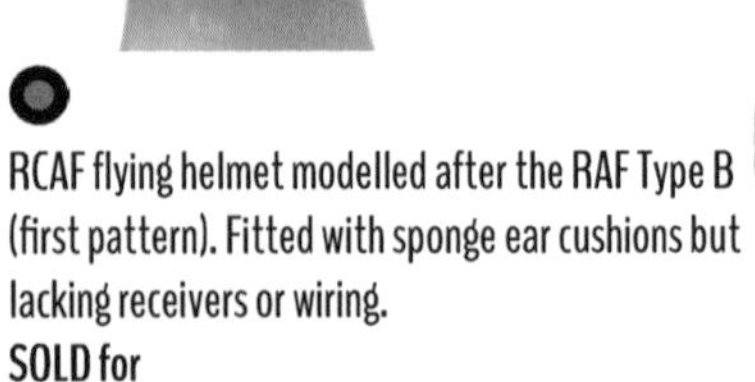

RCAF flying helmet modelled after the RAF Type B (first pattern). Fitted with sponge ear cushions but lacking receivers or wiring.
**SOLD for**
**$307 / £200 / €215**

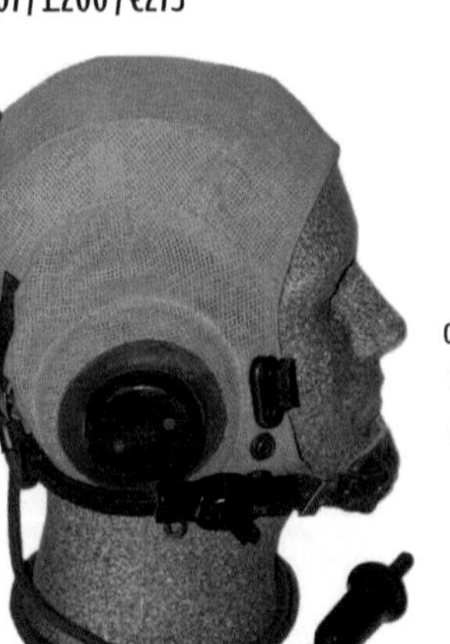

WW II Canadian RCAF summer flying helmet, constructed of cotton mesh similar to the RAF Type E helmet, but fitted with a leather chin cup and an external wiring harness that attaches to the outside of the helmet by means of a series of snaps / press studs. The wiring includes Canadian made receivers, a plug jack for the mask microphone and RAF style bell plug. Excellent, unissued condition.
**SOLD for**
**$475 / £310 / €425**

WW I RFC Goggle mask, Flying, Mk II by Triplex Goggle mask & Lens Co. Ltd. Stores ref. 22C/11. Marked with War Department broad arrow and 'A', and dated AUG 17. One lens broken with missing section.
SOLD for
$452 / £295 / €405

WW II RAF Lightweight flying goggles (commonly referred to as Mk II). Light grey frames marked "Made in England", clear lenses. Good springs in the leather covered strap.
SOLD for
$ 452 / £295 / €405

Pre-WW II commercial / private purchase flying goggles by Theodore, utilising an early RAF style leather strap with steel springs.
SOLD for
$299 / £195 / €268

WW II RAF classic 'Battle of Britain' Mk IIIA pattern goggles. Good condition but both frame 'stops' are missing.
SOLD for
$445 / £295 / €414

WW II RAF Mk IIIA goggles in excellent condition and dated 1935, fitted with tinted celluloid lenses.
SOLD for
$450 / £298 / €420

Excellent set of WW II RAF Mk IIIA pattern goggles dated 1939.
SOLD for
$445 / £350 / €414

WW II RCAF Mk III goggles. Stores Ref. 22/397. Classic 'Battle of Britain' style goggles, Canadian made with RCAF stamp and 1942 date.
SOLD for
$431 / £280 / €378

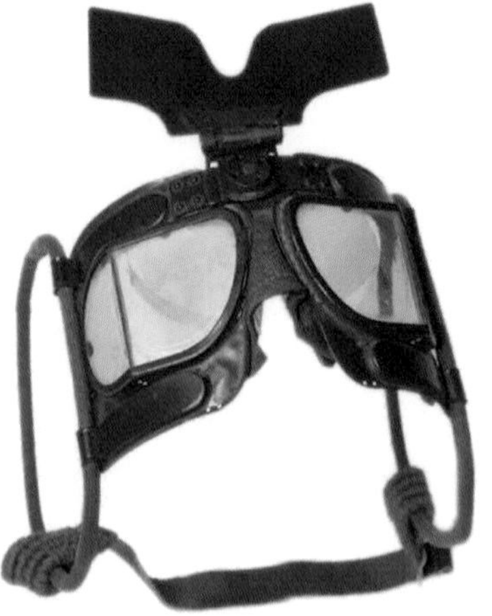

RAF MK IVB goggles complete with the rare and seldom found sun shield. Excellent strap and loop arrangement with the strap clearly marked 22C/167 and the manufacturer's name, Fleming. Black rubber pads are hard with some loss to the rubber. The lenses have delamination but are not cracked.
SOLD for
$482 / £320 / €452

WW II RAF Mk IVB flying goggles, boxed and complete with accessories. Original cardboard box of issue contains goggles in excellent condition fitted with flip-shield / anti-glare screen and a smaller box with a tube of Everclear, frame key/spanner plus a set of helmet plates for attaching to B or C type helmets using the copper rivets provided. The leather/chamois forehead protection strip completes the outfit.
SOLD for
$1008 / £655 / €885

RAF Battle of Britain Period MK IVB goggles. A very good original example with some minor dents, although no evidence of ever having been issued. No flip up sun screen present. Pads have hardened and minor delamination to both lenses.
SOLD for
$302 / £200 / €282

Complete Accessory Kit for Mk IVB goggles comprising brown leather case with four spare lenses, take down tool, Everclear demisting stick, leather brow strip for attaching to helmet for extra comfort, guide plates, copper rivets and additional take down tool in original card box. Lenses have de-laminated, everything else in unissued condition.
SOLD for
$377 / £250 / €353

Luxor 12 goggles by E.B. Meyerowitz. Made famous by the iconic photograph of Pilot Officer Keith Gillman on the cover of Picture Post in August 1940.
Cushions hard / rigid.
SOLD for
$423 / £275 / €372

RAF Mk VII flying goggles. Early pattern with leather strap, in excellent original condition,without flip-up sun screen.
SOLD for
$500 / £325 / €440

RAF Mk VIII flying goggles, wartime manufacture with rolled edge to frames, stores reference 22C/930 stamped on central nose pad. Fitted with tinted lenses and complete with issue box .
**SOLD for**
**$184 / £120 / €165**

RAF Mk VIII goggles in exceptional condition and complete with original box. An unusual variant featuring a rectangular wire hinge. The strap retains full elasticity.
**SOLD for**
**$284 / £185 / €254**

RAF Mk VIII flying goggles, wartime manufacture with rolled edge to frames. Excellent condition and with clear A-crown-M stamp. Stores reference number 22C/960.
**SOLD for**
**$284 / £185 / €254**

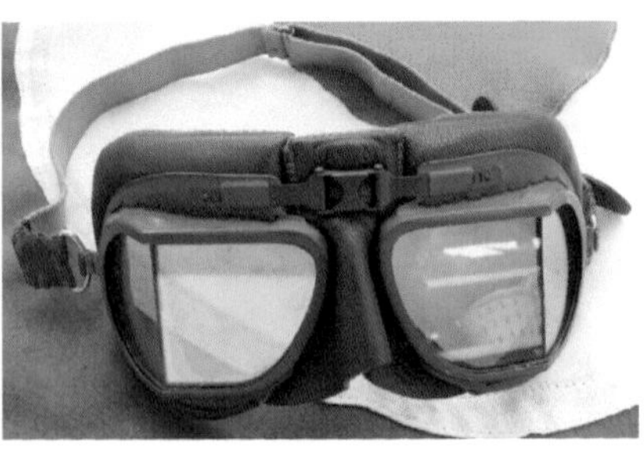

Postwar RAF Mk VIII flying goggles. Stores Ref. 22C/930. Very good condition except the strap which is stretched out and faded.
**SOLD for**
**$92 / £60 / €82**

WW II RAF night training goggles. Black rubber frames, curved glass lenses.
**SOLD for**
**$46 / £30 / €41**

RAF anti-glare spectacles with case. Generally good condition. Frames, springs and leather shields show little sign of wear. Stress fracture in the right lens.
SOLD for
$115 / £75 / €103

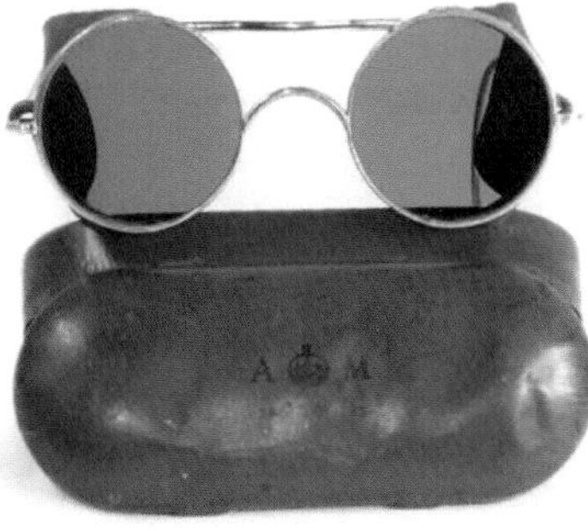

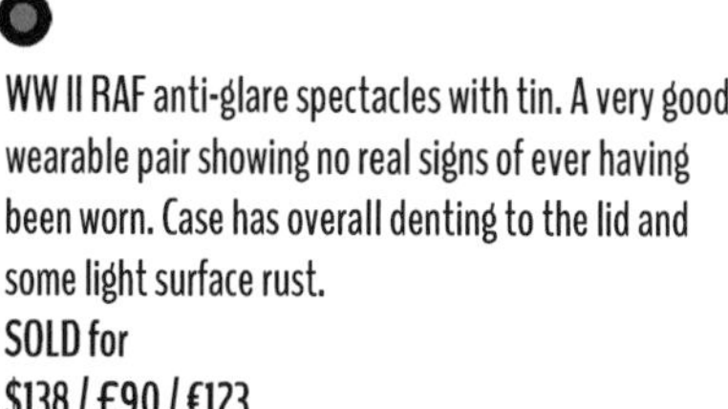

WW II RAF anti-glare spectacles with tin. A very good wearable pair showing no real signs of ever having been worn. Case has overall denting to the lid and some light surface rust.
SOLD for
$138 / £90 / €123

WW II RAF issue Mk VIII anti-glare spectacles/ sunglasses with grey/green tinted lenses in steel wire frames. In very good, wearable condition.
SOLD for
$ 77 / £50 / €69

WW II RAF Mk VIII anti-glare spectacles complete with velvet lined case as issued and in excellent wearable condition.
SOLD for
$138 / £90 / €123

WW II RAF Mk X anti-glare spectacles. 22C/1039. With green acetate side shields in velvet lined case of issue. Maker-marked 'BAO' (British American Optical).
SOLD for
$421 / £275 / €378

An original and scarce RAF Type D oxygen mask, fitted with original type E microphone assembly with wiring loom and plug but without receivers. Replica oxygen tube with original Mk IIIB connector (6D/101)
**SOLD for**
**$3542 / £2350 / €3317**

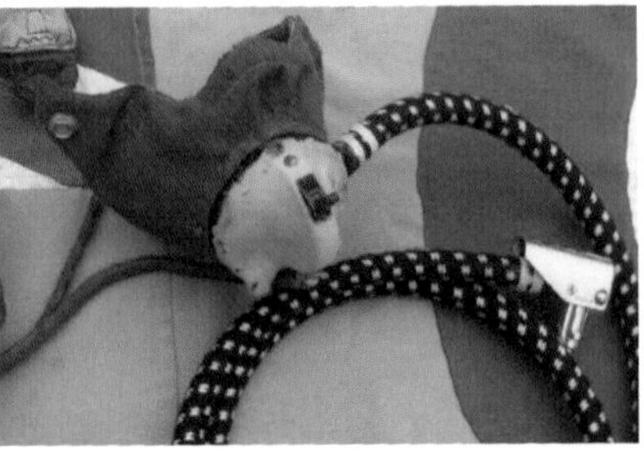

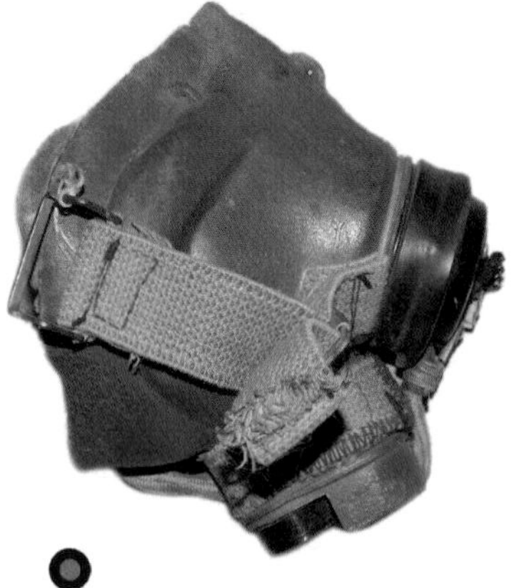

WW II RAF Type G oxygen mask in very good, used condition, with minor splits along the edge, but no signs of perishing to the rubber. Type 48 microphone installed. Lacks nosewire, but no evidence that it has pulled through so may never have been fitted.
**SOLD for**
**$550 / £365 / €515**

Excellent, early example of the RAF Type G oxygen mask fitted with original Type 48 microphone moulded in green rubber and in unissued condition.
**SOLD for**
**$950 / £630 / €884**

WW II RAF Type G oxygen mask in excellent condition, complete with breathing tube and early, external wiring loom fitted with bell-shaped jack plug and telephone receivers.
**SOLD for**
**$894 / £600 / €830**

WW II RAF Type G oxygen mask Stores Ref. 6D/644. Size small and fitted with an excellent type 48 microphone assembly. The rubber is in very good supple condition, and the overall shape is excellent. This mask has probably never been used.

SOLD for
$754 / £500 / €706

A scarce wartime dated example of the RAF Type H oxygen mask, complete with breathing tube and connector. Overall condition of the mask and hose is very good with no cracking or crazing evident. Dated 3/45 the mask is a size medium and is fitted with a quick-disconnect for high-altitude.

SOLD for
$369 / £245 / €346

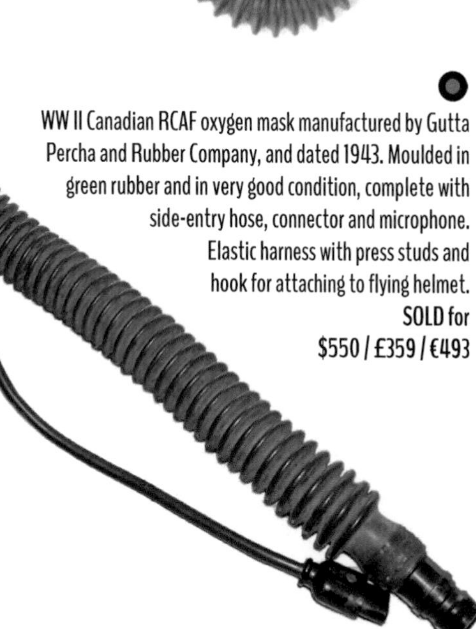

WW II Canadian RCAF oxygen mask manufactured by Gutta Percha and Rubber Company, and dated 1943. Moulded in green rubber and in very good condition, complete with side-entry hose, connector and microphone. Elastic harness with press studs and hook for attaching to flying helmet.

SOLD for
$550 / £359 / €493

WW II RAF breathing tube for a Type D oxygen mask. 36" black rubber tubing with a braided fabric covering of black flecked with yellow and complete with Bayonet Union Mk IIIB connector.

**SOLD for**
**$1200 / £795 / €1117**

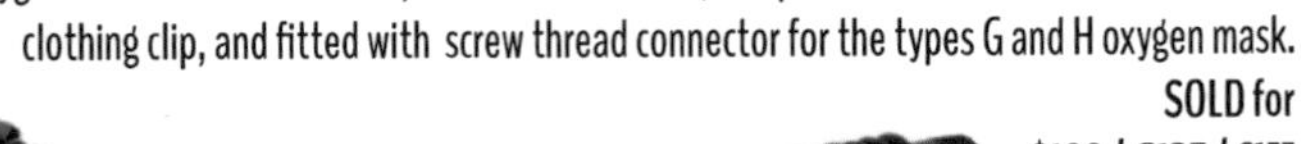

RAF Oxygen Mask Tube in excellent, near mint condition, complete with bayonette connector and clothing clip, and fitted with screw thread connector for the types G and H oxygen mask.

**SOLD for**
**$189 / £125 / €177**

RAF Oxygen Mask Tube of the early, narrow type, complete with bayonette connector and clothing clip. This narrow type tube was fitted to RAF Type E, E* and early production G masks. This example is fitted with a plastic screw connector for the G mask.

**SOLD for**
**$245 / £165 / €228**

WW II RAF flat hook for attachment of Type E*, G and H oxygen mask to flying helmet. Includes nuts and bolts for securing through snap fasteners on right side of helmet.

**SOLD for**
**$58 / £38 / €54**

Mid tan coloured loom with attached 2 pin plug (10H/14206) and large 'bell' jackplug. The 2-pin plug connects to the oxygen mask lead. Suitable for all internally wired Type C, D and E helmets. Unused condition.
SOLD for
$92 / £60 / €82

WW II RAF Type Q cord without plug or receivers fitted. External loom for Type B helmets, also used for early Type C, D and E helmets. Unused, brand new.
SOLD for
$106 / £70 / €99

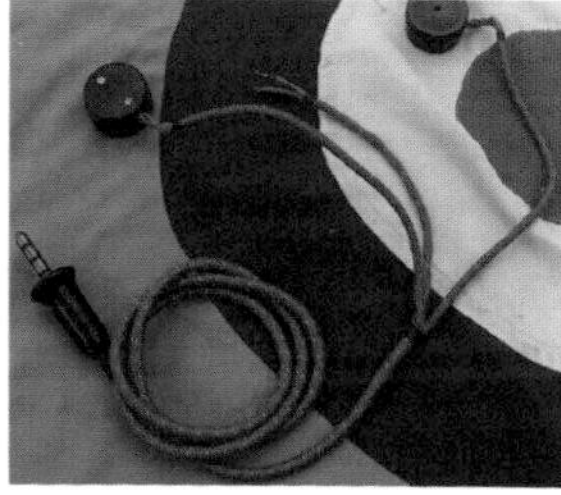

A similar WW II RAF Type Q cord (wiring loom) fitted with plug and receivers. External loom for Type B helmets as well as early Type C, D and E helmets. Good used condition.
SOLD for
$106 / £70 / €99

WW II RAF hinged end or blanking cap for the Type D oxygen mask, used in transit and when microphone not fitted to mask. Black lacquered aluminium covered with chamois. Very good condition.
SOLD for
$50 / £34 / €47

Similar WW II RAF hinged end cap for the Type D oxygen mask, used in transit or when the mask is worn without a microphone. Excellent condition.
SOLD for
$98 / £65 / €92

WW II RAF Type 20 Microphone 10A/11994 (when fitted with Type Q cord, it is known as the Type 21 microphone assembly). Introduced in October 1940 to replace the iconic Type 19 microphone assembly on the Type D oxygen mask. Wiring cut, otherwise in good, used condition.
SOLD for
$144 / £95 / €134

A similar WW II RAF Type 20 Microphone in very good condition, without dents and with all lettering and numbering distinct. Some evidence it may have been repainted at some time.
SOLD for
$181 / £120 / €169

WW II RAF replacement / spare webbing and leather harness for the Type E* oxygen mask.
SOLD for
$100 / £67 / €94

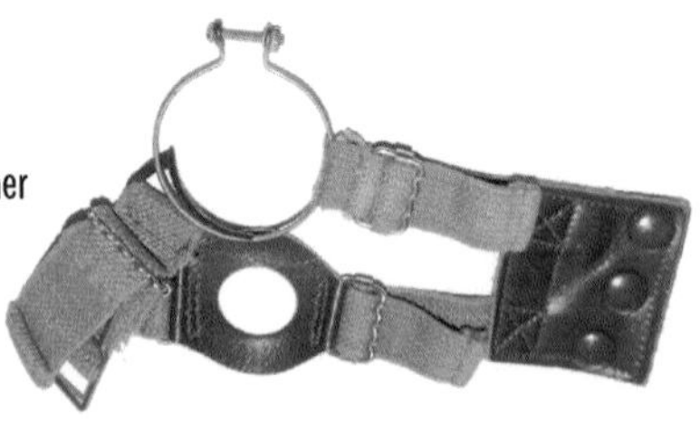

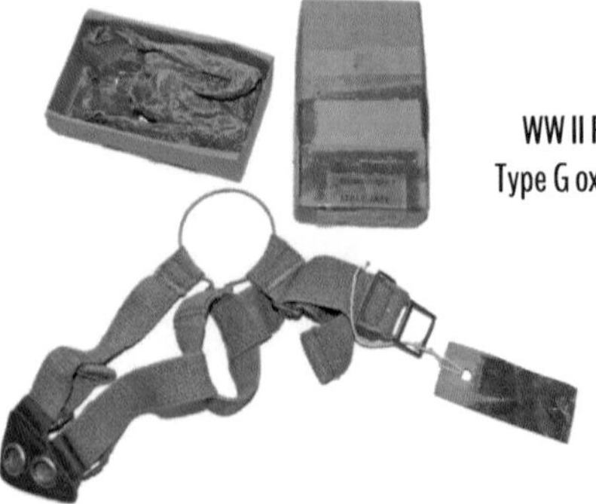

WW II RAF replacement / spare webbing harness for the Type G oxygen mask, contained in its original box of issue.
SOLD for
$85 / £57 / €80

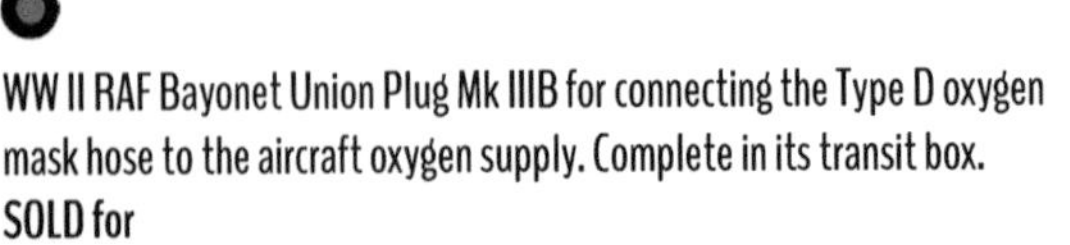

WW II RAF Bayonet Union Plug Mk IIIB for connecting the Type D oxygen mask hose to the aircraft oxygen supply. Complete in its transit box.
SOLD for
$130 / £85 / €120

WW II Luftwaffe model LKpW100 flying helmet. Sheepskin lined leather helmet with all communications gear (round throat microphones), long cord and beehive style plug. Black lacquered alloy earphone housings; friction buckle fastening for the throat microphone strap. Excellent condition.
SOLD for
$750 / £481 / €689

WW II Luftwaffe model LKpS100 flying helmet. Cloth helmet lined with brown silk and complete with all communications gear (round throat microphones with friction type adjustment strap), long cord and beehive style plug. Brown lacquered alloy earphone housings. Excellent condition.
SOLD for
$1203 / £800 / €1110

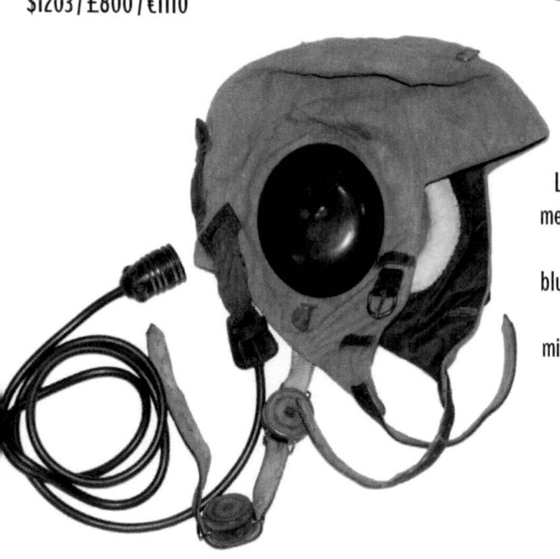

Luftwaffe model LKpS100 summer flying helmet dated 1937 and 1939. Brown cotton cloth with blue satin lining, metal earphone housings and built in throat microphones (strap / buckle type fastening). Overall good, used condition with rust to metal fittings and general wear, but complete.
SOLD for
$750 / £499 / €692

WW II Luftwaffe model LKpN101 lightweight mesh flying helmet (Netzkopfhaube), with chestnut brown leather receiver housings and complete with all communications gear (round throat microphones) including short cord. Second model, configured for use with either 2 or 3 strap oxygen masks. Overall very good, used condition with no damage to netting.
**SOLD for**
**$440 / £281 / €395**

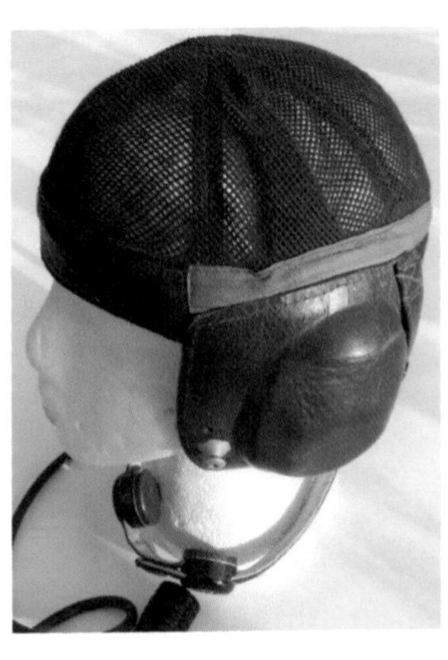

Luftwaffe LKpN101 Netzkopfhaube Flying Helmet with dark brown leather receiver housings and all communications equipment. Type with attachment points for 2-strap oxygen mask only and long cord with plug. Good condition with no damage to netting. Size 55
**SOLD for**
**$460 / £300 / €412**

WW II Luftwaffe model LKpW101 winter flying helmet. Brown leather shell is in excellent condition and still supple. Lamb's wool interior lining shows some use commensurate with use. Metal buckles and oxygen mask clips show none of the normal tarnishing or rust. Avionics complete and helmet is fitted with round Mi4C throat microphones
**SOLD for**
**$500 / £325 / €440**

WW II Luftwaffe model LKpW101 winter flying helmet ir extra large size 60. Dark brown leather with sheepskin lining, complete with all communications gear (oval throat microphones). Overall excellent condition.
**SOLD for**
**$526 / £350 / €485**

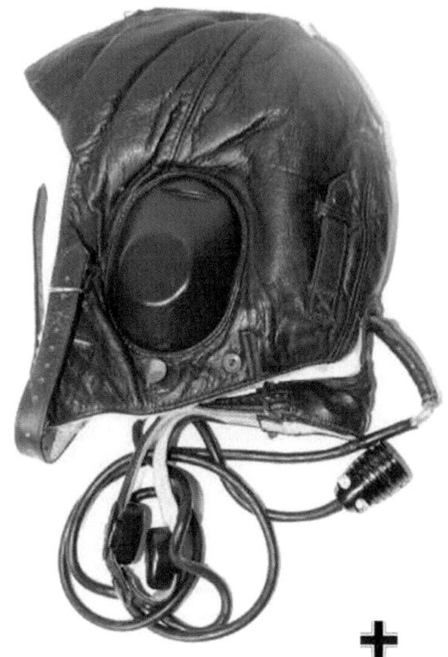

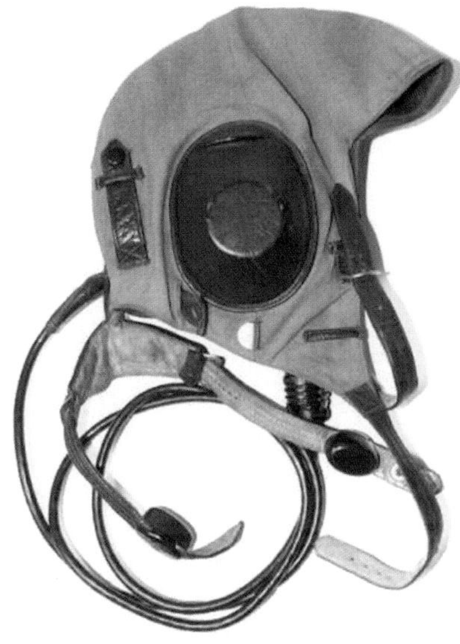

WW II Luftwaffe model LKpS101 summer flying helmet retaining all communications gear with oval throat microphones. Very good, used condition.
**SOLD for**
**$496 / £330 / €458**

WW II Luftwaffe model LKpS101 summer flying helmet from the Battle of Britain period, complete with all communications gear (round throat microphones) and dated 1940. Overall good, used condition.
**SOLD for**
**$400 / £260 / €351**

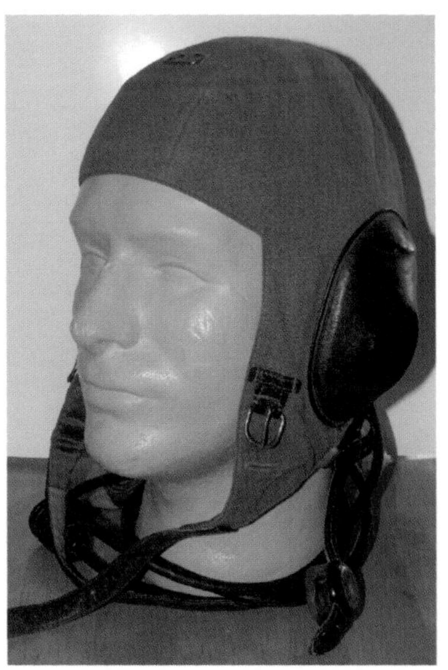

Luftwaffe model LKpS101 summer flying helmet in large size 59, complete with all communications gear (oval throat microphones). Overall very good, used condition.
**SOLD for**
**$526 / £350 / €485**

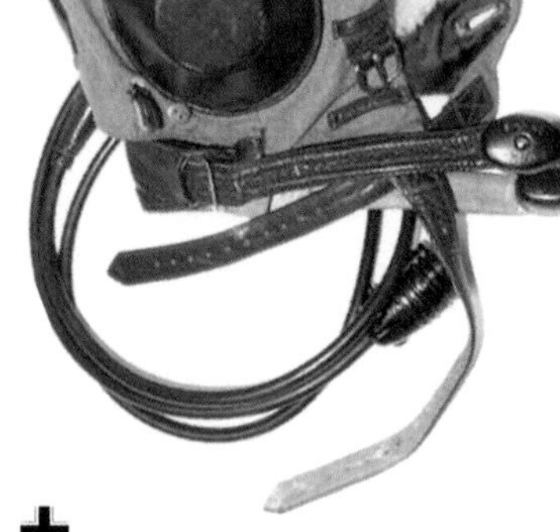

WW II Luftwaffe flying helmet extension lead. Used on both the long and short cord helmets to extend the movement of aircrew within the aircraft.
**SOLD for**
**$125 / £81/ €110**

WW II Luftwaffe model 295 flying goggle kit by Auer. Exceptional condition, includes aluminium case with internal compartment housing 2 sets of extra lenses in cloth pouches, spare strap and chin strap. Case is dated 1935.
**SOLD for**
**$650 / £422 / €571**

WW II Luftwaffe model 295 flying goggle kit by Auer. Exceptional condition, complete with aluminium case with internal compartment housing 3 sets of extra lenses in cloth pouches. Includes the rare chin strap. Case is dated April 1937.
**SOLD for**
**$600 / £390 / €527**

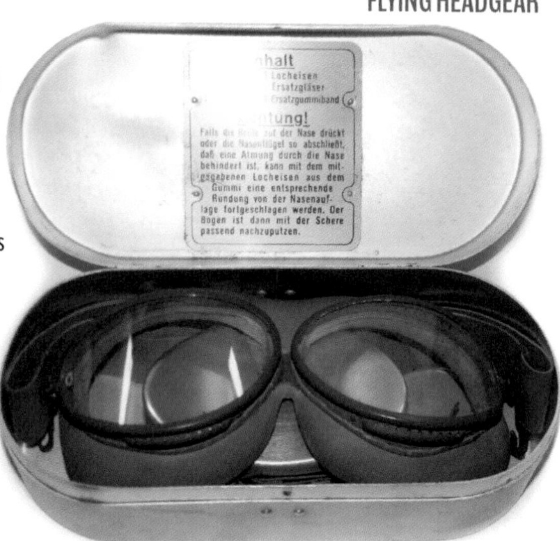

A similarly marked pair of WW II Luftwaffe model 306 flying goggles by Karl Sauer, with grey / green painted plated frames and clear lenses. Very good condition.
**SOLD for**
**$225 / £150 / €213**

WW II Luftwaffe model 306 flying goggles by Karl Sauer, marked G.V.N. and dated 1942. Exceptional condition, with bright nickel plated frames, twin adjustment screws to bridge, dark tinted lenses and dark grey rubber cushions. Standard ribbed elastic strap.
**SOLD for**
**$350 / £221 / €307**

General purpose goggles intended for motor vehicle troops but sometimes pictured being worn by Luftwaffe aircrew. Often confused with Model 306 but lenses are considerably smaller.
**SOLD for**
**$223 / £145 / €196**

Luftwaffe Splitterschutzbrille by Nitsche & Gunther, with rigid frames and fitted with clear lenses and correct grey-green silken elasticated headband. Strap is faded and has lost elasticity. Marked "NiGuRa" and with the size number '2'.
**SOLD for**
**$708 / £460 / €622**

Luftwaffe Model 10-6701 oxygen mask, known as the "fighter bomber" mask. An early example moulded in green rubber and complete with all original straps, tube and crocodile clip, in excellent original condition.
**SOLD for**
**$2250 / £1450 / €2020**

Luftwaffe replacement oxygen mask tube connector for the early Hm 5 / Hm 15 oxygen mask by Draeger. Original pre-WW II or early wartime production stamped with Draeger logo. Nickel plated connector compete with crocodile clip.
**SOLD for**
**$275 / £180 / €250**

WW II Imperial Japanese Army Air Force winter flying helmet. Dark brown leather with rabbit fur lining. Very good condition.
SOLD
$500 / £325 / €439

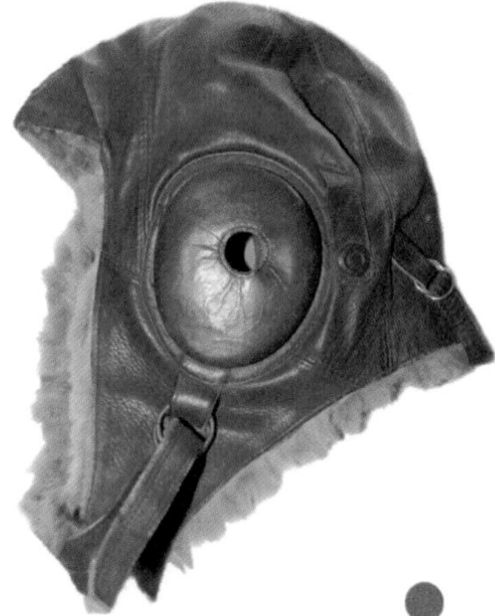

WW II Imperial Japanese Army Air Force flying goggles, contained in their original box together with a velvet lens cloth.
SOLD for
$650 / £422 / €571

WW II Imperial Japanese Army Air Force flying goggles, similar design to the above, in original box with velvet lens cloth.
SOLD for
$679 / £450 / €632

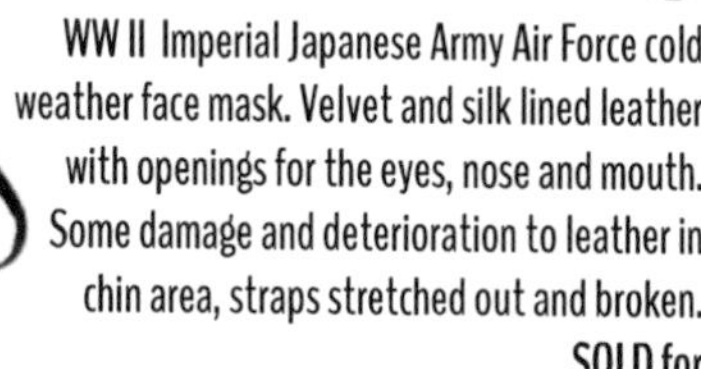

WW II Imperial Japanese Army Air Force cold weather face mask. Velvet and silk lined leather with openings for the eyes, nose and mouth. Some damage and deterioration to leather in chin area, straps stretched out and broken.
SOLD for
$275 / £179 / €242

WW II Imperial Japanese headband. Sometimes incorrectly referred to as a "Kamikaze" headband. Perhaps worn by military personnel for luck and bravery but primarily a "homefront" item.
**SOLD for**
**$30 / £19 / €26**

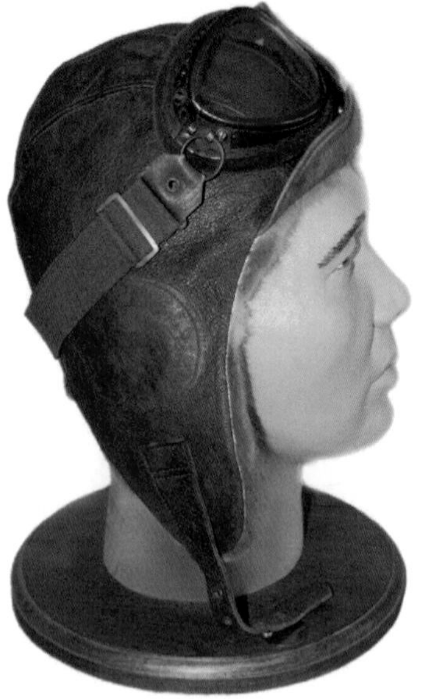

WW II Imperial Japanese Navy Air Force winter flying helmet and goggles, together with a custom made and painted plaster display head mounted on a wood base. An outstanding example of an early wartime fur-lined leather flying helmet retaining both maker's label and official issue tag to interior. Goggles by MAN with lacquered finish and velveteen cushions also in excellent condition, with a small hairline crack to one lens.
**SOLD together as a set for**
**$1330 / £867 / €1192**

WW II Imperial Japanese Navy Air Force flying goggles mask by MAN. Nice example showing very light use.
**SOLD for**
**$750 / £489 / €672**

WW II Italian summer flying helmet, c.1945. Similar pattern and fabric to the RAF Type E but Italian made and equipped with RAF wiring loom and plug for use in allied aircraft. Although of the same basic pattern as the Type E, the mesh is quite different to the British Airtex and the chin strap and leather fittings are also different. Excellent condition.
**SOLD for**
**$575 / £385 / €544**

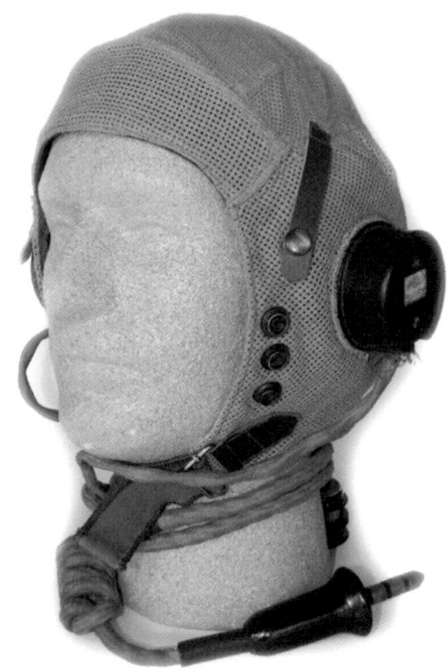

A similar WW II Italian summer flying helmet based on the RAF Type E, complete with RAF wiring loom and plug.
**SOLD for**
**$361 / £242 / €342**

WW II Italian flying goggles with clear glass lenses and amber celluloid flip screens. Flip screens work independently of each other. Marked Brevetto F.O.P.A.I.S.
**SOLD for**
**$450 / £293 / €403**

# FLYING CLOTHING

Flying jackets
Flying suits
Boots
Gloves

WW II US Air Corps / AAF Type A-2 jacket identified to a B-25 crew member with history and a small grouping of other uniform items. Jacket shows wear and use but overall serviceable. Original zip works fine, cuffs shredded. Shoulder patches and leather "chit" removed for post war wear. Theatre made name tag remains to front. Large size (probably 46 chest, though lacks factory label). Sold together with the owner's uniform shirt and service dress tunic, some related paperwork and his named, engraved Air Medal.
**SOLD** as a complete grouping for
**$850 / £569 / €804**

WW II AAF Type A-2 flying jacket, together with an extensive grouping of items relating to Captain Henry H. Day, USAAF, who flew B-24 Liberators with the 380th Bomb Group and completed some 64 Combat missions. Includes his log book, four wartime diaries, wings, dog tags, pilot's navigation kit, leather briefcase and a quantity of photographs plus his 43F year book.
**SOLD for**
**$2265 / £1500 / €2090**

WW II era commercial version of the A-2 jacket. Approximately 40" chest in overall good condition. Talon zip fastener works perfectly. Cuffs and waistband are original to the jacket. Reproduction patch added to match stitch marks on the jacket left by the removal of original.
**SOLD for**
**$187 / £125 / €177**

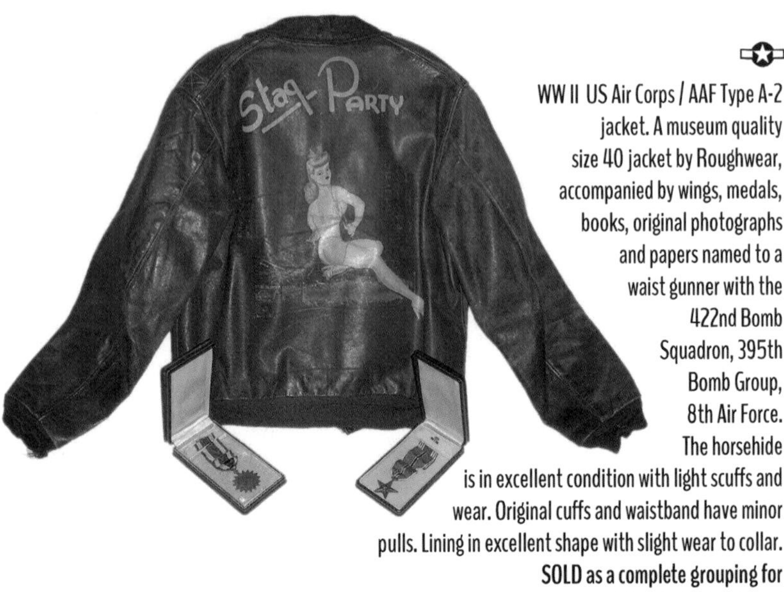


WW II US Air Corps / AAF Type A-2 jacket. A museum quality size 40 jacket by Roughwear, accompanied by wings, medals, books, original photographs and papers named to a waist gunner with the 422nd Bomb Squadron, 395th Bomb Group, 8th Air Force. The horsehide is in excellent condition with light scuffs and wear. Original cuffs and waistband have minor pulls. Lining in excellent shape with slight wear to collar.
**SOLD** as a complete grouping for
**$5100 / £3448 / €4750**

WW II AAF Type A-2 jacket originally belonging to an aviator with the 77th Liaison Squadron, along with other items. The jacket has three multi-piece leather patches made in the China-Burma-India (CBI) theatre and a leather name tag in Chinese. Included with the jacket are six medals: Air Medal, Distinguished Flying Cross, Good Conduct, World War II service medal, Asiatic Pacific Campaign medal and the American Campaign medal. There is also an Army Air Corps Flight School DI, a blood chit, four photographs of the former owner and some of his aircraft and three additional loose patches.
**SOLD** as a large grouping for
**$2300 / £1555 / €2145**

WW II AAF Type B-3 shearling flying jacket by Rough Wear Clothing Co. Size 42, in excellent condition showing light wear and use.
**SOLD for**
**$897 / £600 / €848**

A similar WW II AAF Type B-3 flying jacket. Overall a good, clean example with one or two small repairs.
**SOLD for**
**$636 / £425 / €587**

WW II AAF Type B-10 flying jacket. Designed to replace the A-2 but never as popular, though in reality a far better coat. In very good condition, with original zip fastener. Minor snags to original knit cuffs and waistband. Size 38.
**SOLD for**
**$650 / £435 / €615**

WW II AAF AN-J-4 winter flight jacket by Aero Leather Clothing Co. of Beacon New York. Size 38. Overall appearance is very good although one collar button is missing. AAF decal on the zip flap and remains of a colour AAF shoulder decal. Original 'Conmar' zip slightly damaged close to the bottom and jacket probably best left zipped up.

**SOLD for**
**$785 / £525 / €742**

WW II AAF Type F-1 electrically heated flight suit liner, popularly known as the "bunny suit' because of its blue fleece construction. This example in near perfect, unissued condition.

**SOLD for**
**$600 / £399 / €558**

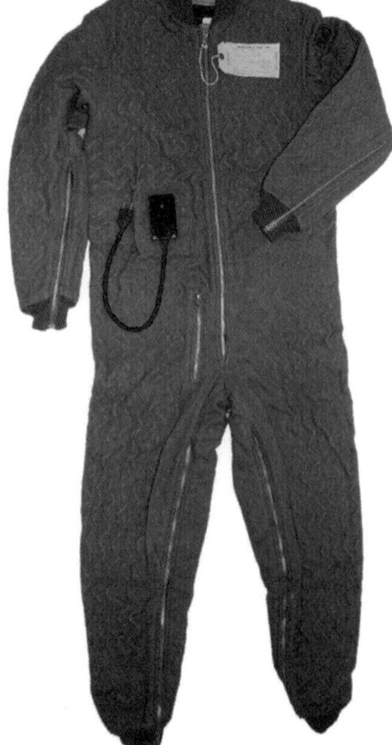

WW II AAF M-2 anti-flak body armour vest (front and back) and M-3 apron. Manufactured by Wilkinson Sword. In excellent condition with minor damage to red felt pull / release tab.

**SOLD for**
**$375 / £250 / €354**

WW II AAF Type A-6A flying boots. Size 11 in near mint condition.
SOLD for
$420 / £280 / €387

WW II USN / USMC Type M422A jacket with history. Rare US Marine Corps name tag to a pilot with VMTB-31 in WW II and continued service through the Korean War. Good, original condition.
SOLD for
$1200 / £250 / €354

Late WW II Irvin jacket with multiple panelled front and rear sections. Faint remnants of white paint on both shoulders (outline of a bomb? Mascot? Too worn to distinguish). One small puncture to leather on the lower right front panel, light surface wear overall. DOT zips may be period replacements. Chain hanger still affixed.
**SOLD for**
**$860 / £575 / €795**

WW II RAF Irvin thermally insulated flight suit trousers in near mint condition, large size and complete with pockets, braces attached and original Air Ministry label attached.
**SOLD for**
**$130 / £415 / €120**

WW II RAF Irvin thermally insulated flying suit trousers Size 4. In fine original condition and complete with braces and original Air Ministry label.
**SOLD for**
**$523 / £350 / €483**

WW II RAF Irvin jacket with painted yellow hood favoured by Coastal Command and Fleet Air Arm crews. Four panel front and rear construction. Very good overall - no tears or repairs just surface wear. Hood retains excellent original paint and flexibility. Original brass DOT main and left sleeve zip. Right sleeve zip missing slider. Label with broad arrow dated 1944.
SOLD for
$890 / £595 / €821

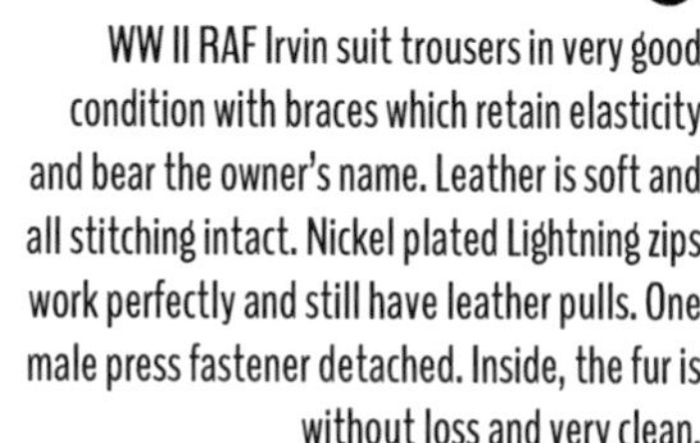

WW II RAF Irvin suit trousers in very good condition with braces which retain elasticity and bear the owner's name. Leather is soft and all stitching intact. Nickel plated Lightning zips work perfectly and still have leather pulls. One male press fastener detached. Inside, the fur is without loss and very clean.
SOLD for
$553 / £375 / €520

WW II RAF Irvin jacket collar strap, black elastic with nickel plated fittings.
SOLD for
$104 / £75 / €113

A similar Irvin jacket collar strap. Similar to the AAF AN6530 goggle strap, used to hold the jacket collar in a raised position around the back of the neck.
SOLD for
$90 / £65 / €98

WW II RAF Type H electrically heated suit lining, size medium, stores reference 22C/1013. One-piece button front full length suit with a simple knitted collar. The electrical supply was taken through a flexible cable (umbilical) with a 3-pin connector/plug. A shorter cable close to the neck supplied power to an oxygen mask heater. The suit had alternative snap connectors at the wrists and ankles to accommodate both 12 and 24 volt power supplies.

**SOLD for**
**$262 / £175 / €242**

WW II RAF 1940 Pattern Flying Suit, known by collectors as the Sidcot Suit. A very good example of the scarce 1940 version, replaced by the 1941 Pattern which was wired to accommodate electrically-heated accessories. Green/ grey waterproof fabric. Overall condition is very good but with a faulty zip to the left leg, small repair to the seat and a split to one button hole in the collar. Zips are a mix of Aero, Lightning and A.M. marked. Detachable collar with owner's name and a good AM stamp.

**SOLD for**
**$435 / £295 / €409**

WW II RAF Sidcot suit collar. Stores ref. 22C/355. Size 3. Technically 'Suits, Flying, 1940 pattern, collar fur, size 3'. Removable collar used with both the 1940 and 1941 pattern Sidcot flying suit.

**SOLD for**
**$55 / £35 / €48**

WW II RAF Type D electrically-heated jacket for use under the Sidcot Suit. The jacket is in excellent condition with a good clear AM marked label.
**SOLD for**
**$222 / £150 / €208**

WW II RAF Suits, aircrew, blouse in a good size 10. All insignia, including sergeant's stripes, have been removed, but the blouse shows no real signs of use and is in very good condition. All original early dished metal buttons are in place and there is a good clear 1943 dated label.
**SOLD for**
**$428 / £290 / €402**

WW II RAF Suits, aircrew, blouse, dated 1943. Often referred to as "Battledress" but issued to aircrews and designed only for wear while flying on operations. Not to be confused with the later issue "War Service Dress" (see uniforms, page 69) which was very similar but issued to all RAF ranks and trades for daily wear. ("Battledress" was strictly army nomenclature). Excellent condition showing very light wear. Includes RAF pilot wing and AM marked ditching whistle.
**SOLD for**
**$325 / £221 / €306**

WW II RAF Suits, aircrew, trousers. Stores ref. 22C/414. Size 8 and 1941 dated - the year of introduction exclusively for wear by aircrews. Flapped front thigh pocket and ankle straps. Early metal buttons throughout. Small moth hole close to the right knee and to the side of the leg.

SOLD for
$333 / £225 / €312

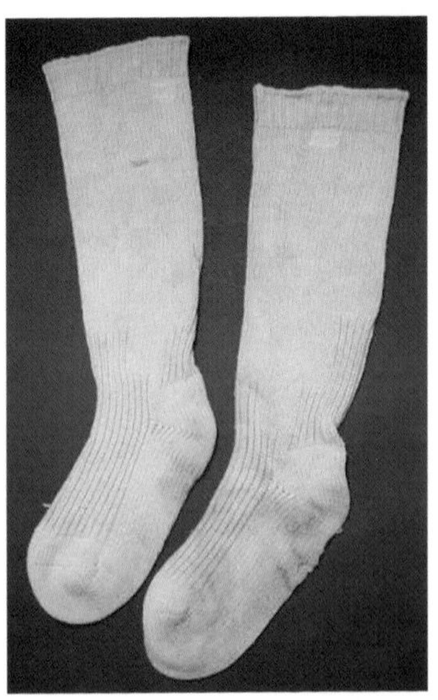

WW II RAF Stockings, white, stores reference 22G/ 2101. General condition is good and ideal for display although they have become rather grey with time, have a few marks and stains from wear and one heel has a hole in it. Both socks have the remains of original labels with stores reference information, made by Lion Brand, size 10 1/2.

SOLD for
$60 / £40 / €56

WW II RAF Royal Aircraft Establishment (RAE) Electrically Heated flying boots 12/24 volt. Size 8. Stores reference 22C/104/163. Brown leather ankle boots with heating elements and a 2-pin plug connector (now removed). The soles and heels show only very light use. A very nice pair of these rare boots.

SOLD for
$522 / £350 / €484

WW II RAF 1936 Pattern Boots dated 1938. A nice pair of these iconic black leather boots in a good size 9 with Air Ministry marked pulls inside. Front soles replaced and surface scratches but no serious damage. Inside, the fur is very good.
SOLD for
$538 / £365 / €504

WW II RAF "Nuffield" boots. Second prototype of the escape boots designed by Christopher Clayton Hutton at MI9, produced under private contract from Lord Nuffield. Chrome leather upper with an offset zip (the first prototype featured a front zip). Good used condition showing normal wear.
SOLD for
$1087 / £725 / €1000

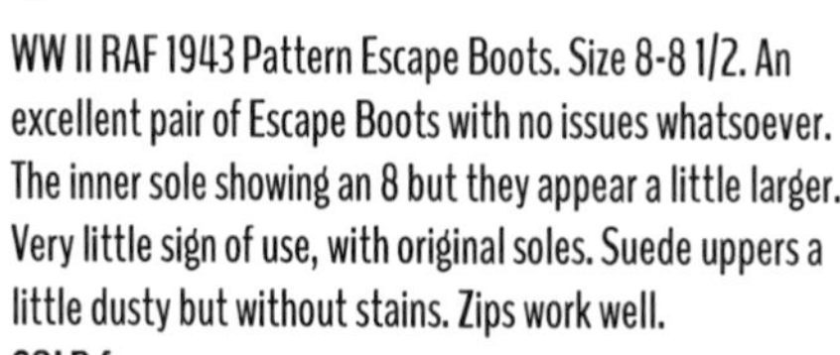

WW II RAF 1943 Pattern Escape Boots. Size 8-8 1/2. An excellent pair of Escape Boots with no issues whatsoever. The inner sole showing an 8 but they appear a little larger. Very little sign of use, with original soles. Suede uppers a little dusty but without stains. Zips work well.
SOLD for
$538 / £290 / €504

WW II RAF 1943 pattern Escape boots with leg uppers removed (shoe section only). This set were found in France, so may have been used as intended!
SOLD for
$187 / £125 / €173

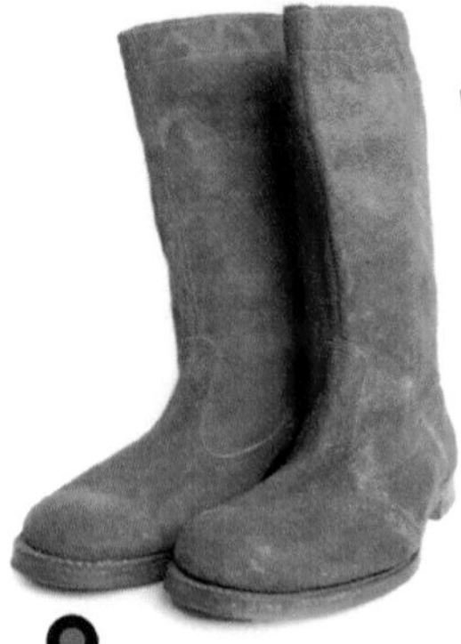

WW II RAF "Mosquito" boots, size 10. Unlined brown suede calf length boots with leather soles in very good condition bar some scuffing. One boot retains the drawstring at the top used to enable a secure fit. Although very popular with pilots and aircrews, these were really intended for ground personnel/wear.

**SOLD for**
**$380 / £250 / €338**

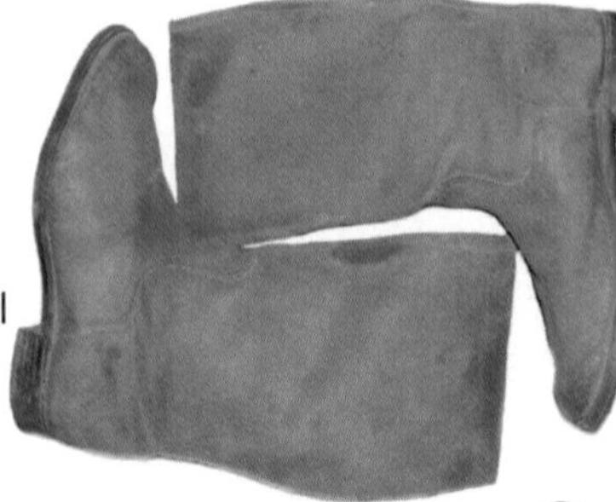

A similar pair of WW II RAF "Mosquito" boots, constructed from green coloured suede. Both lack their drawstring tapes at the top, but remain in overall good, used condition. Size 9 and 1944 dated inside.

**SOLD for**
**$300 / £201 / €277**

WW II RAF flying boot insoles. A matched pair made from leather with sheepskin fur uppers. Size 9, dated 1941 and complete with Air Ministry markings. Show light use.

**SOLD for**
**$28 / £19 / €26**

A similar pair of size 9 WW II RAF flying boot insoles. Matching pair showing light use. One stamped Air Ministry and the other with a broad arrow.

**SOLD for**
**$22 / £15 / €21**

WW II RAF Royal Aircraft Establishment (RAE) Electrically Heated Gloves. Very early issue - for use with the electrically wired Irvin suits. Minor damage to one fingertip and some loss to the suede at the wrist. Good AM stamps at the wrist.

**SOLD for**
**$785 / £525 / €726**

WW II RAF Gauntlets, Flying, 1941 pattern. Diagonal zip flying gauntlets. Stores reference 22C/751/761. Size 8.5. Excellent leather with light use and wear and a fairly good colour match. Air Ministry and A.I.D. markings inside.
**SOLD for**
**$374 / £250 / €346**

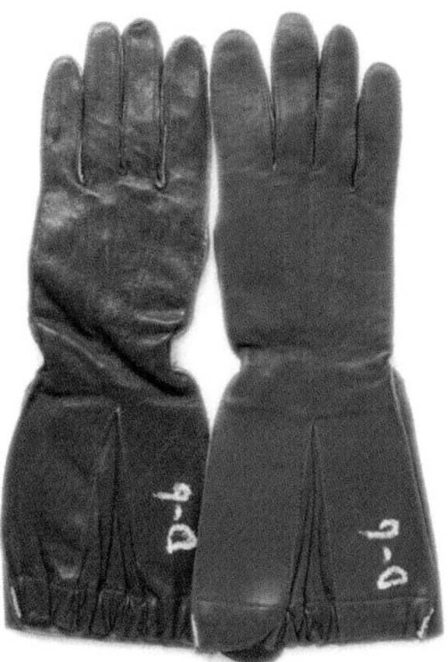

WW II RAF Type D pattern flying gauntlets. Blanket lined leather gloves for wear over the electrically-heated Type D liners. In excellent original condition.
**SOLD for**
**$240 / £160 / €221**

WW II RAF Type D electric flying gauntlet linings by Windak. Stores ref. 22C/716/719, Size large in excellent condition. Intended for use with the Type D leather gauntlets.
**SOLD for**
**$240 / £160 / €222**

A similar pair of WW II RAF Type D electric flying glove liners by Windak for use with the Type D leather gauntlets. Show wear and use but overall good condition.
**SOLD for**
**$135 / £90 / €125**

WW II Luftwaffe flying gloves. The type favoured by fighter pilots whose aircraft had heated cockpits. Unlined grey leather with a short gauntlet and single wrist strap. Unissued condition.

**SOLD for**
**$300 / £202/ €278**

Luftwaffe flying boots. Early wartime double zip pattern with full length zips on both sides of both boots to facilitate easy removal in the event of injury or wound. Later this pattern was replaced with single zip boots to conserve metal for the war effort. Well used and worn with some repairs.

**SOLD for**
**$850 / £545 / €761**

WW II Italian Regia Aeronautica flying outfit, comprising 2-piece flying suit, flying helmet and goggles, all in outstanding condition.

**SOLD for**
**$1120 / £750 / €1035**

# UNIFORMS

Protective helmets
Caps
Tunics and trousers
Coats
Belts
Shirts

WW I USMC steel helmet. Extremely rare and beautifully executed helmet, painted with the eagle, globe and anchor logo front and centre. Leather chin strap and inner wool and leather liner with a twine mesh net.
**SOLD for**
**$1895 / £1288 / €1778**

WW II US Army officer's service dress visor cap by Knox. Small size (approx. 6-3/4 – 7). Olive drab "chocolate" felt cap with mid brown leather bill an front strap, large gilt badge to front.
**SOLD for**
**$230 / £150 / €206**

WW II US Army officer's service dress visor cap. Size 7-1/8. Olive drab doeskin felt cap with mid brown leather bill and front strap, gilt badge to front. Some wear to interior and slight moth damage to crown.
**SOLD for**
**$99 / £67 / €92**

WW II US Army enlisted man's visor cap with mid tan faux leather peak. Two-piece badge, pale yellow satin lining with celluloid name card holder. A little mis-shaped but clean, good used condition.
**SOLD for**
**$82 / £55 / €77**

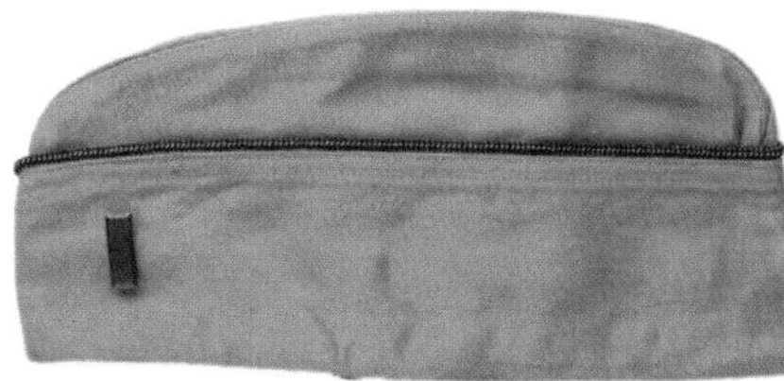

WW II US Army officer's light tan cotton sidecap with black and gold piping, fitted with pin backed sterling 1st Lieutenant bar. Good used condition.
**SOLD for**
**$49 / £32 / €43**

WW I United States Navy overseas tunic with a stunning bullion British-made wing. Named to a probable Silver Star recipient. British tailor-made sewn down Lt. JG shoulder boards, a single overseas stripe and heavily-detailed bullion pilot wing. A great piece of history showing light wear.
**SOLD for**
**$3275 / £2195 / €3028**

WW II US Army officer's dress tunic in dark green gabardine. AAF and CBI shoulder patches. Bullion collar devices and rank bars embroidered directly to fabric. Hash marks to left sleeve. Lacking belt and aircrew wing. Sold together with the owner's A-2 jacket and uniform shirt, some related paperwork and his engraved Air Medal.
**SOLD as a complete grouping for**
**$850 / £569 / €804**

WW II US Army officer's service dress uniform in green gabardine, named and with provenance to a 4th Fighter Group pilot who previously served with the RCAF. Tunic has all insignia including miniature RCAF wings. Sold together with his service dress cap, uniform shirt, tie and trousers, his RCAF pilot's log book with numerous combat entries, and his personal diary detailing his service up to his death in 1944.
**SOLD for**
**$3000 / £2025 / €2090**

WW II RAF Eagle Squadron tunic. One of three tunics named and with provenance to a 4th Fighter Group pilot who served with the RAF Eagle Squadrons. RAF wings and matching Eagle patches to both arms. In excellent condition.
**Set of 3 tunics SOLD for**
**$ 4000 / £2695 / €3728**

WW II US Army officer's service dress uniform in dark green gabardine, lined with red satin, named and with provenance to a 4th Fighter Group pilot who had previously served with the RAF Eagle Squadrons. All insignia including miniature RAF wings present. Note: the 1942 RAF badge to the right pocket is a replacement. Sold as part of a grouping with 2 earlier RAF Eagle Squadron tunics belonging to the same pilot.
**Set of 3 tunics SOLD for**
**$ 4000 / £2695 / €3728**

WW II US Army officer's service dress tunic, summer weight, in khaki / tan cotton. With AAF shoulder patch, sterling USAAF pilot wing and miniature RAF wing, named and attributed to a former member of the Eagle Squadrons.
**SOLD for**
**$250 / £169 / €233**

WW II US Army officer's shirt, most probably made in the CBI theatre. Heavy cotton shirt has captain's bars, branch of service insignia (winged prop) and aircrew wing embroidered directly to fabric. Sold together with the owner's A-2 jacket and uniform shirt, some related paperwork and his engraved Air Medal.
**SOLD** as a complete grouping for
**$850 / £569 / €804**

WW II United States Navy lieutenant's aviation uniform, comprising jacket and pants. The jacket is unnamed and has a bullion wing.
**SOLD for**
**$115 / £78 / €107**

WW II RAF Regiment Mk II Helmet. Amongst the rarest of British helmets and appears unissued. Excellent gold RAF Regiment decal. Original mid war "Pea Green" paint. Liner shows no signs of use and fibre band is marked with the size, 7, manufacturer's initials G & S and the date 1942.
**SOLD for**
**$370 / £250 / €345**

Early WW II or possibly pre-war RAF officer's cap in very good condition with the Regent Street outfitters label still attached to the lining. Clean soft sweatband impressed "Real Roam Leather". Size 6 3/4. Underside of peak is dark green.
**SOLD for**
**$274 / £185 / €255**

Early WW II RAF officer's cap by Burberry, named and identified to a pilot and DFC winner. A few small moth nips to the crown and underside of the peak. Fitted with a faded but heavily padded bullion badge.
**SOLD for**
**$259 / £175 / €242**

RAF Officer's service dress cap as issued to NCOs promoted through the ranks from about 1943, fitted with a scarce economy type badge with a metal crown.
**SOLD for**
**$274 / £185 / €255**

Wartime pattern RAF serge beret dated 1945. A virtually mint example of the 1943 pattern beret, famously photographed being worn by RAF glider pilots before Operation Varsity. Not to be confused with the post war wool Berets.
**SOLD for**
**$74 / £50 / €69**

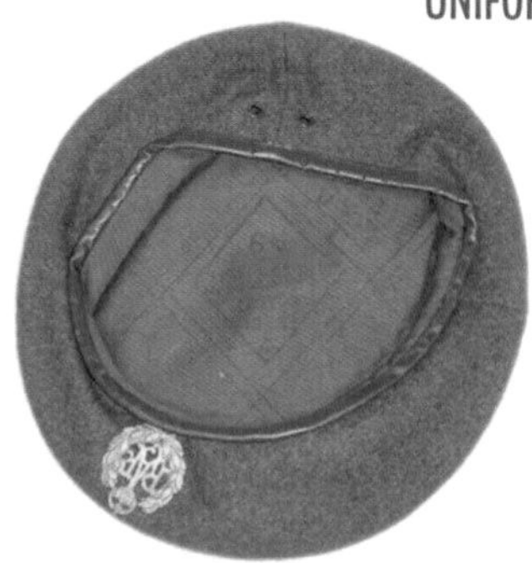

WW II RAF Wolseley helmet, better known as a pith helmet. Condition is good with some mottling and one small cut to the material on the left side of the peak. Original RAF puggaree (flash) shows mothing. WD stamp inside.
**SOLD for**
**$ 185 / £125 / €173**

WW II RAF officer's side cap, issue pattern in blue barathea lined with blue ribbed silk. Complete with gilt 2 piece badge and gilt RAF buttons. Very good condition with light wear.
**SOLD for**
**$60 / £41/ €56**

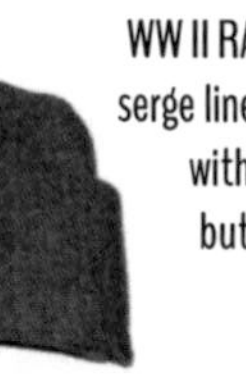

WW II RAF other ranks' side cap in blue serge lined with black cotton and fitted with stamped brass cap badge and buttons. Broad arrow marked and dated 1943.
**SOLD for**
**$50 / £34 / €47**

WW II RAF officer's side cap. Standard pattern, privately made by H. R. Bloomfield and dated 1944, but never fitted with a badge!
**SOLD for**
**$ 111 / £75 / €104**

RCAF officer's side cap by The Hamilton Uniform Cap Company Ltd. Standard Canadian manufacture side cap in barathea cloth, identical to a British made example bar the buttons.
**SOLD for**
**$97 / £65 / €90**

WW II RAF officer's field service cap to an officer of Air rank (Air Commodore and above) by Gieves of Bond Street, London. Heavily padded bullion badge and sky blue piping. Light wear overall.
**SOLD for**
**$437 / £295 / €407**

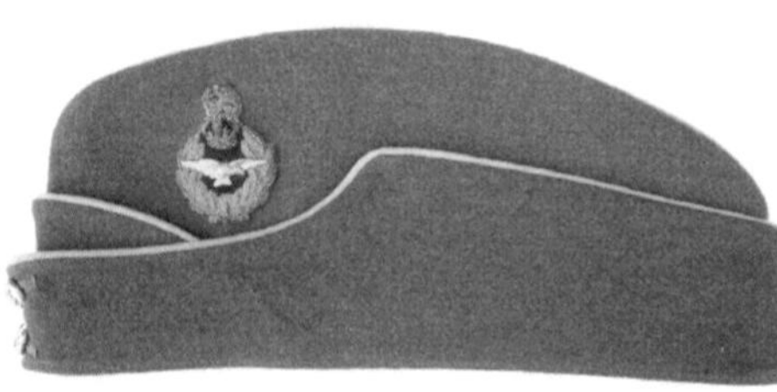

World War I Royal Flying Corps officer's field service cap. General Service buttons to front and bronze RFC badge with a cotter pin upon the left side. Hall Bros., Oxford manufacturer label inside.
**SOLD for**
**$475 / £320 / €440**

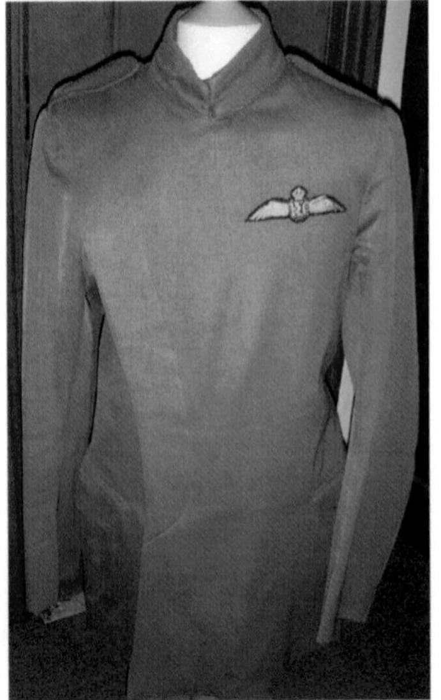

WW I Royal Flying Corps maternity tunic. Named tunic has a beautiful 4" embroidered wing and Royal Flying Corps shoulder flashes. There are hidden snaps at the shoulders to fasten the plastron front portion that hides the buttons beneath. This tunic still has its original Silvers of Reading tailor's label with the original wearer's name written inside. Rear vent and inside pocket. Great condition.
**SOLD for**
**$3675 / £2470 / €3408**

RAF horizon blue officer's tunic. Extremely rare 1918-1919 Royal Air Force service dress uniform jacket in sky blue, with bullion pilot wing and WW I ribbon bar. Only worn for a very short period, this uniform jacket was quickly phased out and replaced with the more familiar blue-grey. Rear vent and wool lining beneath the collar. Great condition.
**SOLD for**
**$4675 / £3160 / €4355**

WW II RAF War Service Dress blouse (not to be confused with the earlier "Suits, Aircrew", see page 55). A very good example, showing almost no signs of use with excellent pilot wings. WD inspector's stamp with the letter "L" indicates 1946 issue.
**SOLD for**
**$260 / £175 / €242**

RAF War Service Dress Blouse and Trousers. 1945 dated set in excellent condition and good display size 7. Both items carry the same owner's name.
**SOLD for**
**$328 / £220 / €304**

WW II British made War Service Dress blouse and Suits Aircrew trousers, issued to a navigator with 431 Squadron on Halifax and later Lancaster aircraft. Leather name tag over right breast pocket and original miniature escape compass button, still in place on the right shoulder strap. Canada shoulder titles and large RCAF half wing. Burton's label with clear 1944 date (trousers dated 1943). Sold with copy photographs and a copy of the owner's log book.

**SOLD for**
**$1042 / £700 / €965**

WW II RAF officer's khaki drill tunic for tropical use. Fitted with detachable shoulder boards to the rank of Flying Officer with VR tabs, and a very nice set of heavily padded pilot wings with a sewn on, pin-back brass backing plate so they could be detached for cleaning. Excellent condition.

**SOLD for**
**$250 / £168 / €233**

WW II RAF officer's khaki drill tunic and trousers for wear in tropical regions. Showing clear evidence of pilot wings having been worn at some time, and fitted with a very good pair of detachable shoulder boards. Each collar has two holes where badges, possibly VR or perhaps medical / dental branch insignia were affixed at some time. Tunic chest size about 38" with a trouser waist 33".

**SOLD for**
**$179 / £120 / €165**

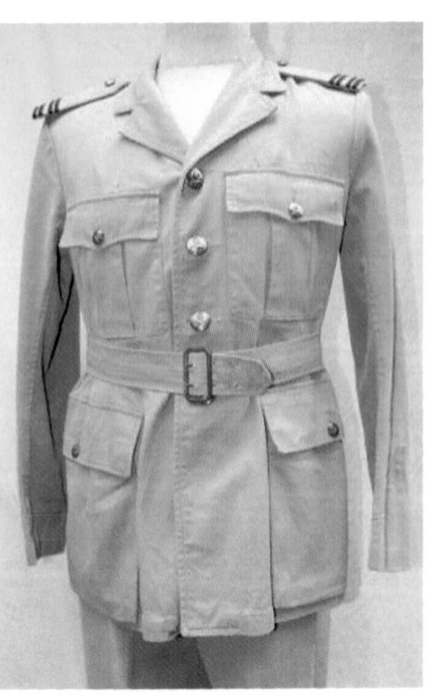

WW II RAF Greatcoat by the well-known British maker, Crombie. Approximately 38" chest, the coat is in very good condition. The interior is part lined with a quilted material and all buttons, and belt, are in place. There are no shoulder boards and no indication of any having ever been fitted. The original chain hanger is in place as is the Crombie label but there is an additional Toronto tailor's label in an inside pocket. Presumably these coats were imported for RAF graduates in Canadian Training Schools.

**SOLD for**
**$140 / £95 / €130**

WW II RAF Shirt with separate collar. 1943 dated RAF collarless shirt, pullover version with the two buttons (replaced) and one collar stud opening. Made by Faulat in Belfast.

**SOLD for**
**$178 / £120 / €166**

WW II RAF other ranks shirt and collar. Shirt with the short, two button and collar stud opening. 40" chest and approximately 15" separate collar. Very good with no damage or staining and missing only one sleeve button. Collar clearly marked with the manufacture's stamp and 1945 date.

**SOLD for**
**$178 / £120 / €166**

Luftwaffe model M 1935 double decal steel helmet in original untouched condition.
**SOLD for**
**$ 1342 / £875 / €1203**

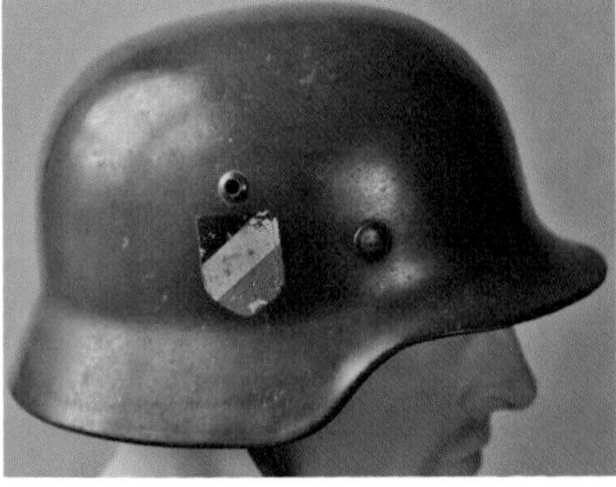

Luftwaffe officer's cap showing lots of use and wear with light stains, but without serious damage. Well made bullion insignia including the smaller, early eagle. An early cap, made by Erel.
**SOLD for**
**$ 750 / £506 / €699**

A very good early Luftwaffe officer's cap, featuring the attractive wire insignia and the smaller droop tail eagle. Very good with no sign of any damage, just light use. Classic saddle shape with a steeply angled peak, the green backing of which is smooth, suggesting pre-1936 manufacture. Grey silk lining with celluloid moisture shield intact showing clear Berlin retailer's details.

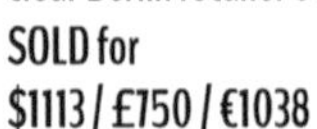

**SOLD for**
**$1113 / £750 / €1038**

WW II Luftwaffe enlisted man's M-43 field cap in good used condition. Two front buttons. Both insignia sewn to wool backing.

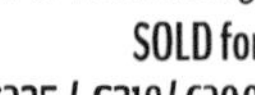

**SOLD for**
**$325 / £218/ €300**

WW II Luftwaffe enlisted man's overseas cap, most likely made in France. The front of the cap has an embroidered wing and the national cockade, and has black piping / Waffenfarbe for the engineering branch.
**SOLD for**
**\$200 / £135 / €185**

WW II Luftwaffe enlisted man's overseas cap with eagle and national cockade on blue wool. Well used and personalized inside, but no damage.
**SOLD for**
**\$275 / £185/ €255**

1939 dated Luftwaffe belt and buckle. Wear to the high points of the aluminium buckle but overall very good condition showing minimal use. Buckle marked RS&S (Richard Sieper & Sohne), Tab marked LBA along with a manufacture's stamp date of 1939.
**SOLD for**
**\$177 / £120/ €166**

Luftwaffe belt buckle and tab by F.W. ASSMAN & SOHNE in unissued, unused condition, retaining original factory paint and lacquer with just the smallest amount of paint loss to the high point of the eagle's right wing.
**SOLD for**
**\$177 / £120/ €166**

Luftwaffe officer's service dress shirt in blue grey cotton, worn with the Waffenrock or Fliegerbluse while on operational duty. Could also be worn alone and has provision for detachable shoulder boards. Nice machine sewn eagle and pressed paper buttons. Large size. Shows light use only.
**SOLD for**
**$350 / £236 / €326**

Luftwaffe officer's tropical shirt in heavy tan cotton, worn with the tropical uniform tunic or on its own, and includes provision for detachable shoulder boards. Eagle has been carefully removed leaving a triangular stitching pattern. Large size. Shows light use only.
**SOLD for**
**$300 / £203/ €280**

A similar Luftwaffe officer's service dress shirt in blue grey cotton. Provision for detachable shoulder boards and fitted with plastic buttons. Shows use and some light staining, eagle removed carelessly leaving a small tear to front. Large size.
**SOLD for**
**$125 / £85 / €117**

# LIFE JACKETS / PARACHUTES

Life jackets
Parachutes
Parachute harnesses
Storage bags
Accessories

WW II US Navy / Marine Corps Mk I "wrap-around" live saving vest. In very good condition, the rubberized canvas is supple and the original oral inflation tubes are still present.
**SOLD for**
**$900 / £615 / €850**

AAF Type B-5 life preserver or "Mae West". Post war example in unissued condition, with leg tapes still tied and taped as it left the factory, complete with accessories including dye marker, signal mirror and shark chaser pouch.
**SOLD for**
**$99 / £68 / €94**

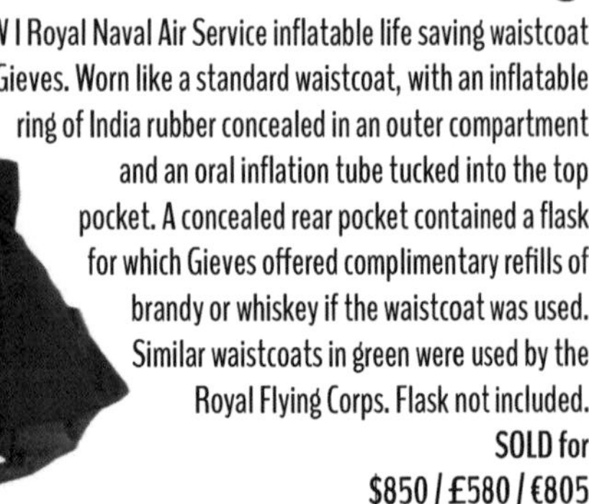

WW I Royal Naval Air Service inflatable life saving waistcoat by Gieves. Worn like a standard waistcoat, with an inflatable ring of India rubber concealed in an outer compartment and an oral inflation tube tucked into the top pocket. A concealed rear pocket contained a flask for which Gieves offered complimentary refills of brandy or whiskey if the waistcoat was used. Similar waistcoats in green were used by the Royal Flying Corps. Flask not included.
**SOLD for**
**$850 / £580 / €805**

WW II RAF / RCAF 1932 pattern life saving waistcoat. Canadian made version of the Battle of Britain issue pattern "Mae West." Yellow fabric with rubberized compartment containing original stole (bladder) and kapok pads. Excellent condition with good label and clear instructions stamped to front of lobes.
**SOLD for**
**$1000 / £682 / €945**

WW II RAF 1941 pattern RAF life vest, complete. With stole (bladder) dated 4/43, kapok pads and inflation mechanism including CO2 cartridge (inert). Condition is very good with a nice label and clear Air Ministry Stamp.
**SOLD for**
**$1247 /£850 / €1180**

A similar WW II RAF 1941 pattern life vest retaining all of the leg straps, grab handles, tying tapes and buttons. Fitted with correct kapok pads but lacking inflatable stole and inflation lever. Clean label with broad arrow.
**SOLD for**
**$506 / £345 / €479**

A similar WW II RAF 1941 pattern life vest. Stores ref. 22C/447. Size medium in very good condition, retaining all of the leg straps, grab handles, tying tapes and buttons. Lacking stole, inflation lever and kapok pads. Labeled with War Department broad arrow markings.

**SOLD for**
**$711 / £485 / €673**

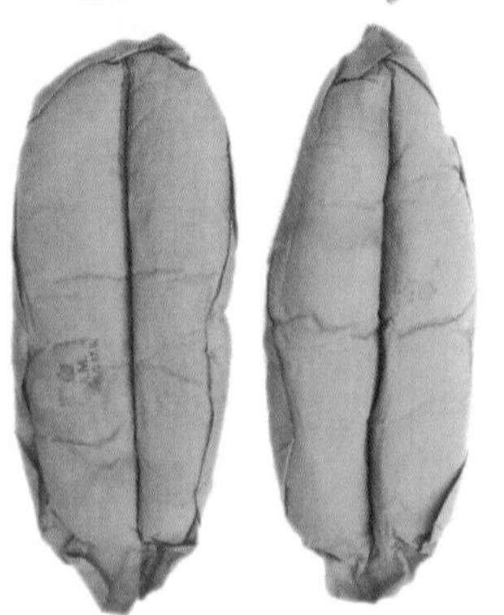

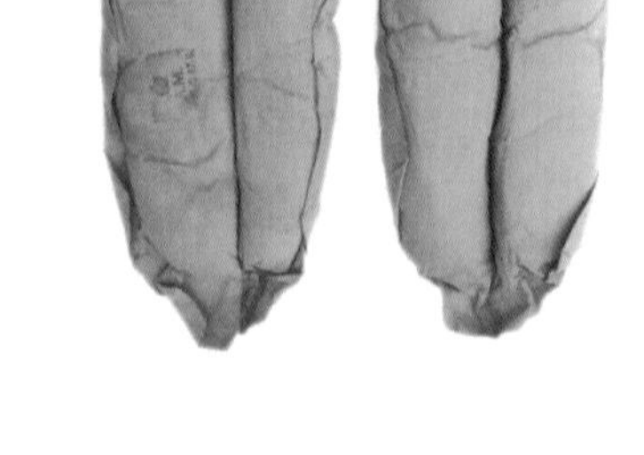

WW II RAF 1941 pattern life vest kapok pads, set of three. Air Ministry marked and in excellent condition.

**SOLD for**
**$330 / £225 / €313**

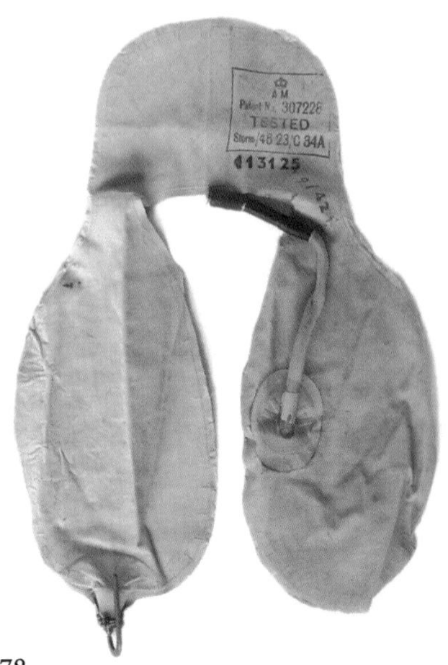


WW II RAF 1941 pattern life vest stole (bladder). Stores ref. 22C/72. Grey rubberized cotton, fitted with a circlip and an inflation lever which is heavily pitted and has lost its plated finish. Air Ministry marked and with 9.42 manufacture date.

**SOLD for**
**$265 /£180 / €250**

WW II Luftwaffe model 10-30 life vest or Schwimmweste with known history and provenance. Extremely rare early production in bright red rubberized canvas. Taken from a Me 109 pilot shot down over Norway in May 1940 by local fishermen who rescued him from the water. Includes a letter of provenance with details.
Dated 1937.
**SOLD for**
**$3721 / £2400 / €3340**

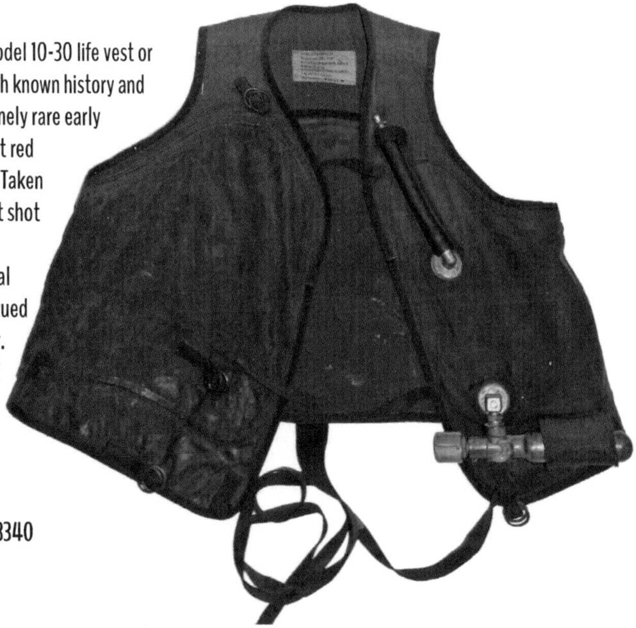

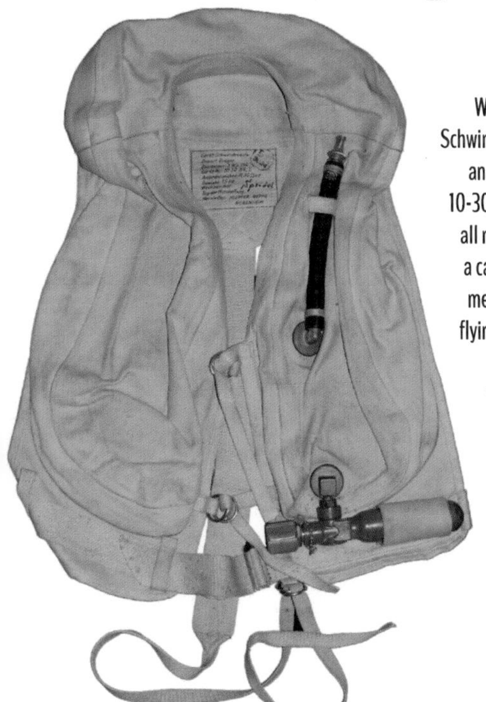

WW II Luftwaffe model 10-30 B life vest / Schwimmweste with significant known history and provenance. The 10-30 B replaced the 10-30 model in 1941. This early example with all metal plated fittings was liberated from a captured German crewman and used by a member of the RAF Eagle squadrons while flying with the RAF and USAAF. German life vests were considered prizes by allied fighter pilots because of their cartridge inflation. Sold with a letter of provenance. A rare piece of history!
**SOLD for**
**$4000 / £2721 / €3784**

WW II AAF / USN seat type parachute model AN6510-1 by Switlik Parachute Company, dated 1942. Standard issue parachute with spring clip fittings, complete with harness, pack, silk canopy, D-ring and seat cushion. Small hole in cushion, otherwise excellent condition.
**SOLD for**
**$1150 / £747 / €1010**

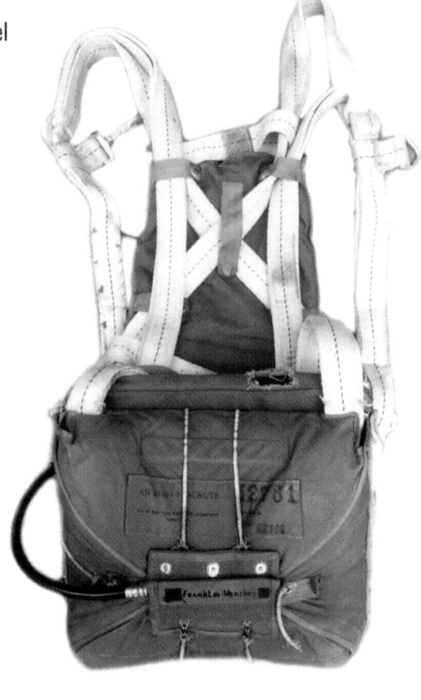

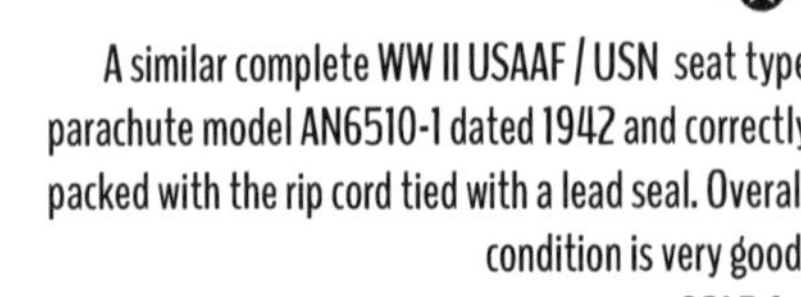

A similar complete WW II USAAF / USN seat type parachute model AN6510-1 dated 1942 and correctly packed with the rip cord tied with a lead seal. Overall condition is very good.
**SOLD for**
**$1644 / £1100 / €1557**

WW II USAAF / USN seat type parachute, part number 35N1115-2 by Pioneer Parachute Co., dated March 1942. Early style with twist clip fastenings. Complete parachute with harness, pack, silk canopy, D-ring and leather seat cushion. Good, used condition.
**SOLD for**
**$ 1200 / £780 / €1054**

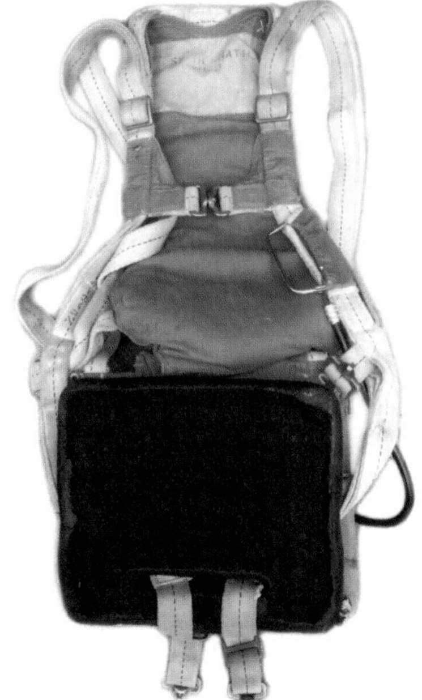

WW II AAF / USN aviator's kit bag AN6505-1. Usually referred to as a "parachute bag" though intended to carry all flying clothing and personal equipment.
**SOLD for**
**$45 / £29 / €40**

A similar WW II USAAF / USN aviator kit bag Type AN6505-1. The original owner wrote his name on one of the handle straps. This bag has a early Talon zips and there is a small lock on one zipper but the key has been lost.
**SOLD for**
**$ 125 / £85 / €118**

WW II RAF seat type parachute, Type S Mk 2 made by Irvin Air Chute Co. A very early example with the less common "C" shaped seat cushion. Includes webbing harness, pack, seat cushion and back pad plus D ring and cord but no silk. Well used and stained from storage but a rare example.

**SOLD for**
**$2465 / £1650 / €2336**

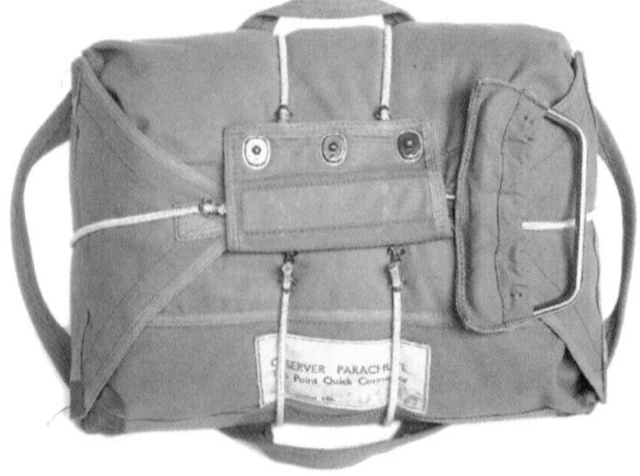

WW II RAF observer type parachute pack manufactured by G.Q. Complete with all webbing grab handles, D-ring and cord. Contains partial silk canopy.

**SOLD for**
**$1000 / £650 / €879**

WW II RAF observer type parachute harness, 1944 dated, Canadian manufacture, with both harness and back pad marked Irvin Air Chute Company (IAC). The harness is in near excellent condition with heavily nickel plated hooks and buckles. The shaved edge to the quick release buckle is most likely a later modification (for the wearer to determine correct orientation at night or in poor visibility). These were issued RAF and all commonwealth crews. The pad is good bar a small area of damage to one edge.

**SOLD for**
**$ 1195 / £800 / €1130**

WW II RAF Harness Suit by Irvin Air Chute Company. A virtually mint condition example of the dual purpose Irvin Harness Suit, size large with a clear date of 25 Sept 1940. No harness is present but both early spring clips for attaching the chest pack parachute remain. These are extremely rare and finish the suit off perfectly for display. All zips work perfectly and all the early dished brass buttons remain.

**SOLD for**
**$1077 / £720 / €1018**

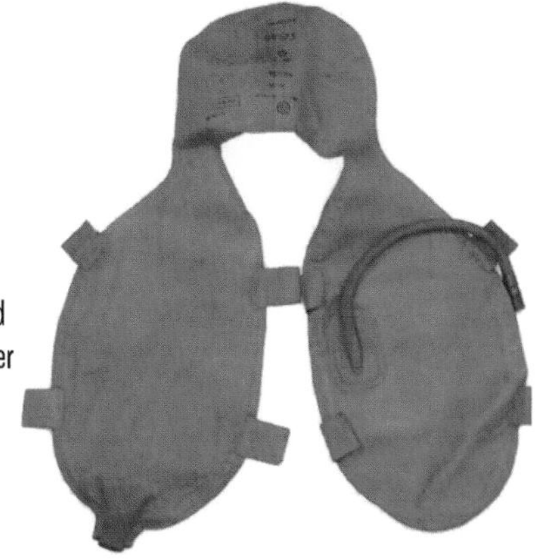

Correct bladder (stole) for the above Irvin Harness Suit. In very good condition and profusely stamped with inspection dates, the earliest being September 1940. No lever or air bottle present.

**SOLD for**
**$314 / £210 / €297**

WW II RAF seat type parachute cushion. In virtually as new condition, and the Sorbo rubber pad still soft. All four tabs and fasteners are in place and both AM and AID stamps are clear and distinct.

**SOLD for**
**$225 / £150 / €212**

WW II RAF 24-panel parachute canopy. Used with both seat type and observer parachute packs. Canopy and rigging lines appear to be in good condition but missing three lines. Air Ministry marked with AID stamp and serial number.

**SOLD for**
**$458 / £306 / €434**

WW II RAF parachute bag. Used for storage of parachutes and other personal equipment.
SOLD for
$123 / £80 / €110

RAF post war seat type parachute, Mk 2. Stores reference 15A/683. This parachute was designed for use with the Martin Baker Mk 2C series ejection seat as fitted to Canberra aircraft.
SOLD for
$539 / £350 / €473

RAF post war seat type parachute Type S Mk4 dated 1954. In very good overall condition and virtually identical to the wartime pattern with the obvious exception of the black buckles on the harness. No parachute canopy, rigging lines or bungee cords. Pack labelled 15A/658. Pad labelled 15A/957.
SOLD for
$897 / £600 / €850

WW II RAF parachute quick release buckle. In overall very good working condition. The release plate has had one edge shaved, a practice introduced later in the war to provide better awareness of the orientation of the buckle.
SOLD for
$113 / £75 / €106

Luftwaffe parachute transit bag used by aircrew and Fallschirmjager. Lightly used condition with all stitching intact, just missing one snap fastener. Stamped with Fl number.
SOLD for
$178 / £120 / €164

Italian seat type parachute harness and pack with all straps and attachments, D-ring and ripcord, but no canopy present. Very good condition showing age and wear but no damage. Matching serial numbers on all components.
SOLD for
$2750 / £1875 / €2601

# ESCAPE / EVASION / SURVIVAL

Escape maps
Escape compasses
Blood chits
Survival and ration kits
First aid outfits
Dinghies and dinghy accessories

WW II USAAF USN pilot / aircrew evasion chart No. 34 (Southeast China) and 35 (Northeast China). Printed two sides in full colour on rayon.
**SOLD for**
**$23 / £15 / €20**

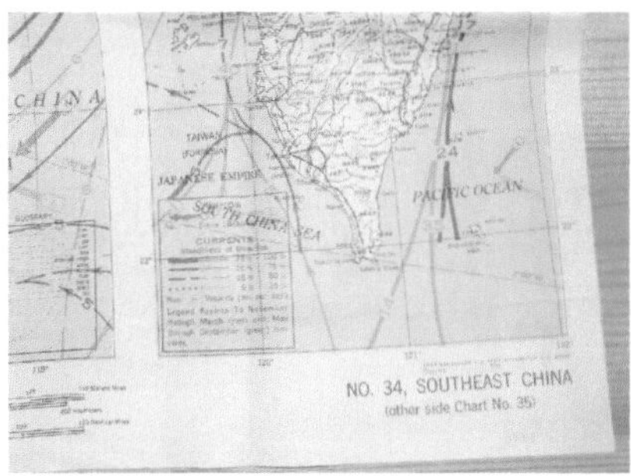


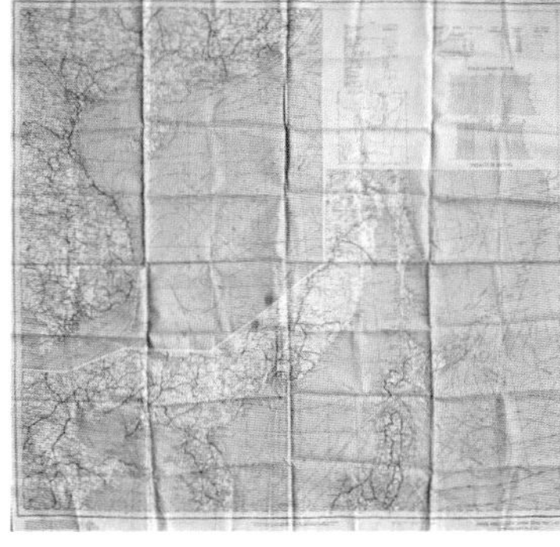

WW II USAAF USN pilot / aircrew evasion charts, sheet C-52 and C-53, Japan and South China Seas. Double sided, 78 x 82 cm. May 1945 dated.
**SOLD for**
**$77 / £50 / €68**

WW II USAAF pilot / aircrew evasion drift chart NACI-HO No. S-12. Drift charts showed currents in summer on one side and winter on the reverse. Printed two sides in full colour on rayon.
**SOLD for**
**$38 / £25 / €33**

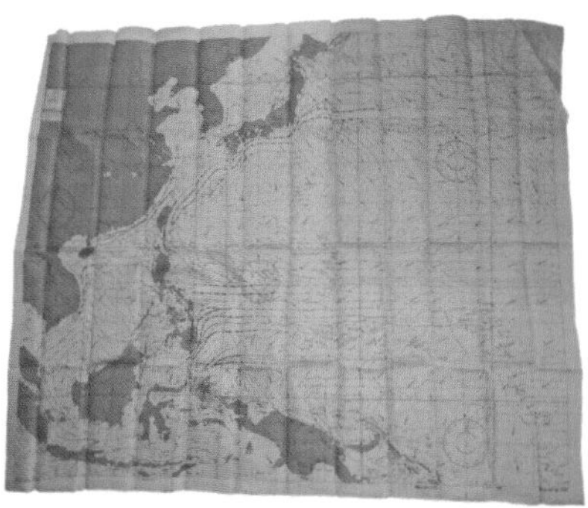

WW II USAAF USN pilot / aircrew evasion charts, Philippine Series, sheet 34 and C-40, Luzon. Double sided, dated April 1944. In excellent condition, folded but no staining or damage.
**SOLD for**
**$51 / £35 / €47**

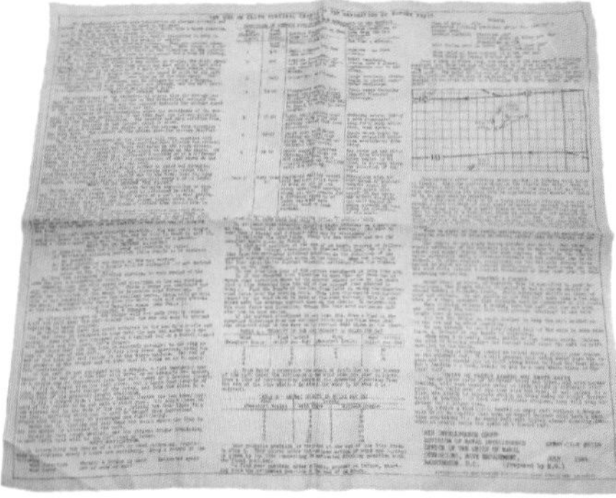

WW II evasion chart instruction sheet. Printed in black, one side only. Gives instruction on how to use the charts. Issued to both AAF and USN pilots and aircrews, this is the Navy version, considered quite scarce.
**SOLD for**
**$34 / £22 / €30**

WW II AAF combination blood chit and escape / evasion map showing the way from K'un-Ming in Yunnan, China to Chabua in Assan, India. In the right hand column, the soldier's friendly message is translated into seven languages. A rare item.
**SOLD for**
**$400 / £272 / €375**

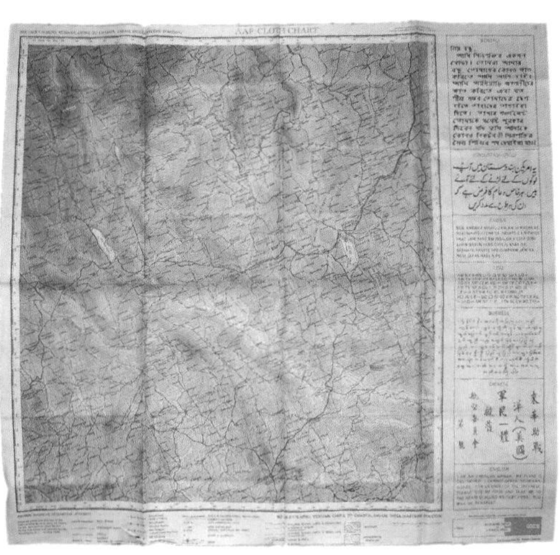

WW II USAAF six language blood chit. Scarce six-language Blood Chit, first made in the US and produced by MIS-X in March of 1944. Languages include: Burmese, Thai, Chinese, Kachin, Lisu and Hindustani.
**SOLD for**
**$300 / £204 / €282**

AVG type blood chit. Extremely rare and possibly unique AVG type Chinese blood chit handmade in leather. The China Air Task Force (CATF) replaced the 1st American Volunteer Group (aka "Flying Tigers") and was the precursor to the 14th Air Force. This chit is possibly from early on in the CATF period, but definitely the 1942 era. Separate pieces of red and blue leather make up the Chinese flag, with a cut-out design for the sun.

**SOLD for**
**$2500 / £1700 / €2345**

WW II AAF Chinese made blood chit dating from mid-late 1942. Still in the larger AVG size (about 7.875"x 10.5") but with the "chop mark" at left instead of centered. Original four digit serial no. (appears to be 1332) stamped out and a low 5 digit no. added. Only two characters next to serial no. (later chits had three). As close as you can get to AVG!

**SOLD for**
**$2000 / £204 / €282**

Mid-World War II AAF blood chit manufactured in China by the Chinese Aero Commission, whose large, red stamped "chop mark" is bottom left of the chit. Near the bottom right are the "May Guo" characters stamped in purple, the phonetic way to say American in Cantonese, which let the reader know that the person possessing the chit was American.

**SOLD for**
**$775 / £521 / €727**

WW II AAF leather blood chit made in the China-Burma-India theatre. Multi-piece leather construction showing US and Chinese flags side by side, with Chinese characters below. No value as an official chit, but worn on flight jackets to communicate goodwill. Initials or maker mark USM on reverse.

**SOLD for**
**$350 / £238 / €329**

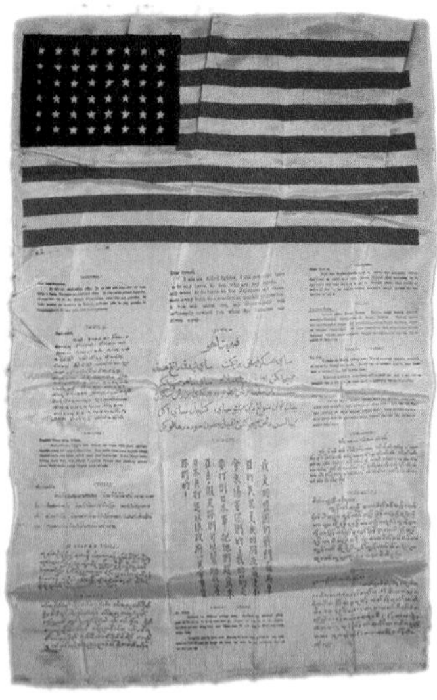

WW II AAF 17 language blood chit. Printed on silk in the China-Burma-India theatre. The American flag sits prominently at the top of the chit and a friendly anti-Japanese-only message has been translated in seventeen languages below.

**SOLD for**
**$275 / £187 / €258**

WW II AAF Emergency Sustenance Vest, Type C-1, manufactured by Breslee Mfg. Co. Commonly known as C-1 survival vest. Good overall condition and complete with all pockets, pistol holster and straps. Repairs to front lower pockets and two webbing straps have been crudely added – one at the neck and one close to the left shoulder. All pockets are labelled for contents. Good AAF label and inspection stamps.

**SOLD for**
**$131 / £85 / €115**

WW II AAF Holster, Plastic, Waterproof for the Type C-1 Emergency Sustenance Vest. This is the holster for the .45 pistol, manufactured from semi transparent flexible plastic. Printed Instructions in blue ink read (indistinctly) 'FOLD ON LINES AND ROLL TIGHTLY CLOSE SNAP'.

SOLD for

$58 / £38 / €51

WW II AAF Spit and Gaff set for the Type C-1 Emergency Sustenance Vest. Manufactured by The American Display Co. of Dayton Ohio. Collapsible steel rod can be used as a weapon, spit or fishing spear when combined with the gaff hook set.

SOLD for

$123 / £80 / €108

A similar AAF Spit and Gaff set for the Type C-1 Emergency Sustenance Vest. Manufactured by The American Display Co. of Dayton Ohio.

SOLD for

$112 / £75 / €103

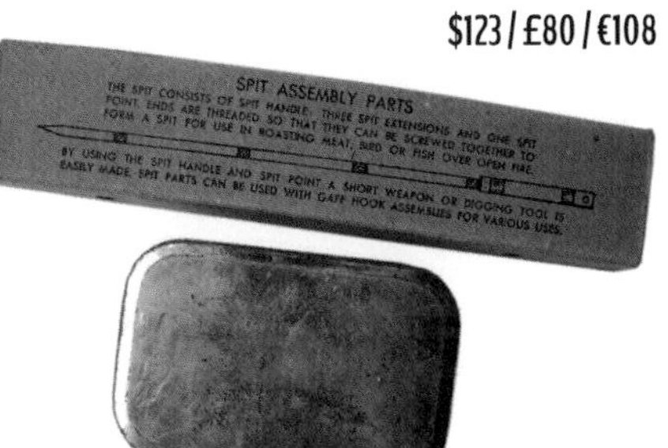

WW II AAF insect repellent for the Type C-1 Emergency Sustenance Vest. A sealed can with all contents still present. A few minor dings and some paint loss but rare to find intact.

SOLD for

$38 / £25 / €34

WW II AAF fishing kit for the Type C-1 Emergency Sustenance Vest. Includes hooks, lines, floats, flies and instruction sheet.

SOLD for

$134 / £90 / €123

WW II AAF Type E3A escape kit. Still sealed with green tape. Overall condition of the container is very good with no cracks or splits. The contents do perhaps show some deterioration.
**SOLD for**
**$482 / £325 / €443**

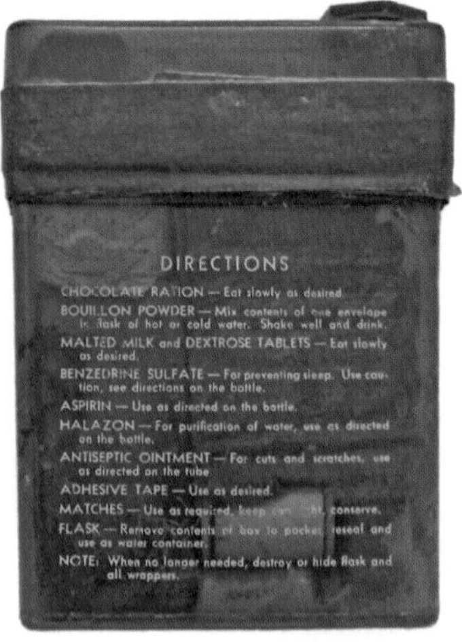

A similar E3A escape kit issued to USAAF aircrews from 1943. All contents present though some show slight deterioration / leakage. Still sealed with heavy green cotton tape.
**SOLD for**
**$270 / £172 / €217**

WW II US Navy aviator's life raft seat pack (AN 6520-1). The pack was manufactured in 1943 by Firestone Tire & Rubber Company. It appears to have been tested during WW II, but was not used and is now dry and fairly hard. **SOLD for**
**$145 / £99 / €137**

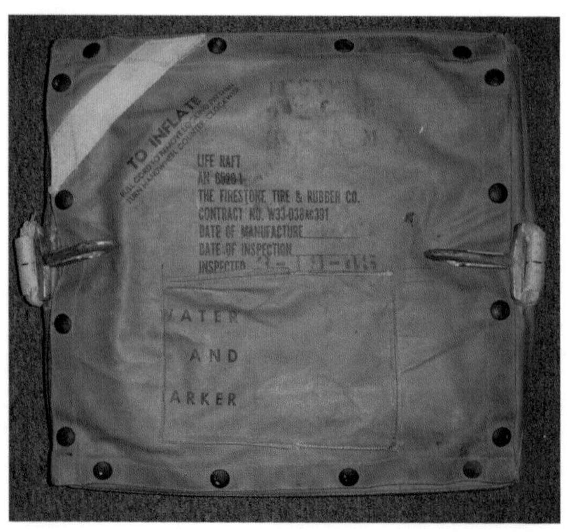

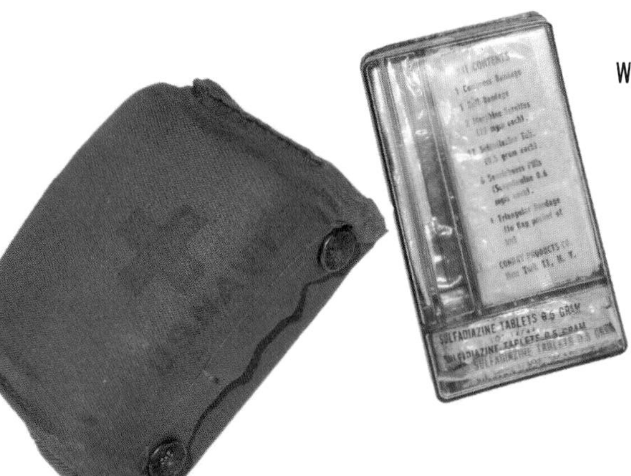

WW II US Navy aviator's personal First Aid Kit with all contents. OD green cotton pouch attaches to belt or parachute harness.
SOLD for
$67 / £45 / €63

WW II Army Air Forces survival guide, covering what to do in emergencies encountered in the jungle, desert, the Arctic and in the ocean. Information ranges from practical advice on how to determine when to bail out of a disabled aircraft to instructions on how to trap a monkey.
SOLD for
$60 / £41 / €56

WW II US Navy escape and evasion kit, more commonly known as the "barter kit". Issued to aviators only in special circumstances, the sealed, hard rubber block contained 15/100 troy ounces of gold in the form of coins and rings.
SOLD for
$900 / £605 / €836

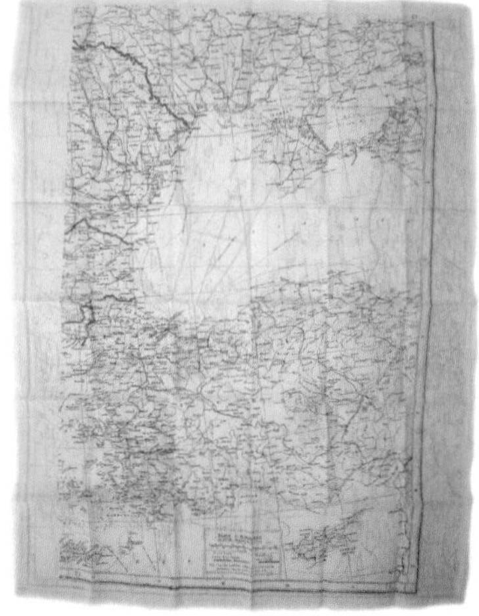

WW II RAF silk / rayon escape / evasion map Sheets T1 and T3. Double sided black and white map showing parts of Russia and Turkey, the Black Sea, Cyprus, Egypt, Syria and Iraq.
**SOLD for**
**$90 / £60 / €82**

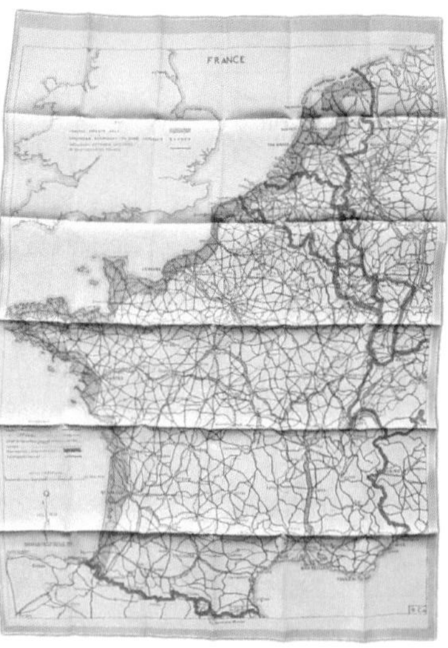


WW II RAF silk / rayon escape / evasion map. Sheet 9.C.(a) / 2.B. Double sided black and white map with colour boundaries and major routes. Approx. 600 mm x 430 mm. Coastal defence area and boundaries of occupied France. An outline of England and Wales to upper left. Reverse is printed in black and features parts of Eastern France, Holland, Switzerland, Germany, Poland, etc.
**SOLD for**
**$112 / £75 / €102**

WW II RAF escape and evasion map. Germany and Scandinavia. An excellent example of a British made evasion map, made available from 1943 onwards. Made of artificial silk with heat-sealed edges. Sheet E covering on one side areas of Germany, Denmark, Sweden, Norway, Finland and the Murmansk area of the USSR and sheet A, covering areas of Sweden and Norway. 870 mm x 780 mm in very good condition.
**SOLD for**
**$82 / £55 / €75**

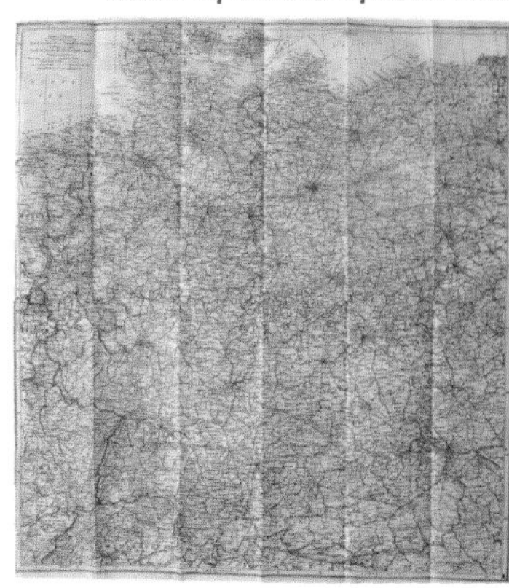

WW II RAF issue tissue paper map, Sheet A. Approximately 47 x 50 cm, single sided, printed in black, red and green ink. Eastern parts of Holland, Belgium and France and borders with Germany, Swiss and Italian borders with Germany, and parts of the North Sea and Baltic. Made of special 'tissue' from pulp seized from a Japanese cargo ship by MI9.
SOLD for
$112 / £75 / €102

WW II fly button escape compasses. 7 pairs (base and magnetized pointer button) still attached to original card, prior to issue.
SOLD for
$275 / £180 / €247

WW II fly button escape compass button set. In excellent condition and still pointing north.
SOLD for
$87 / £58 / €79

WW II RAF Emergency compass as issued in map pouches, escape kits, concealed in buttons etc. First type with four-hole rotary pointer.
SOLD for
$115 / £79 / €108

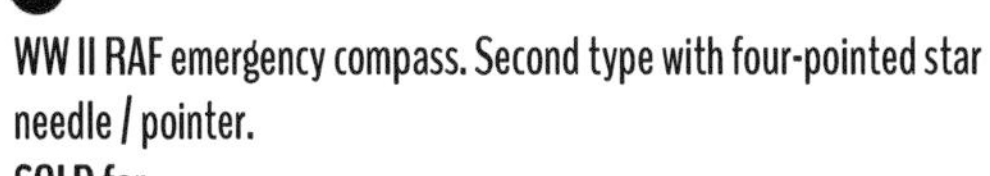

WW II RAF emergency compass. Second type with four-pointed star needle / pointer.
SOLD for
$35 / £22 / €28

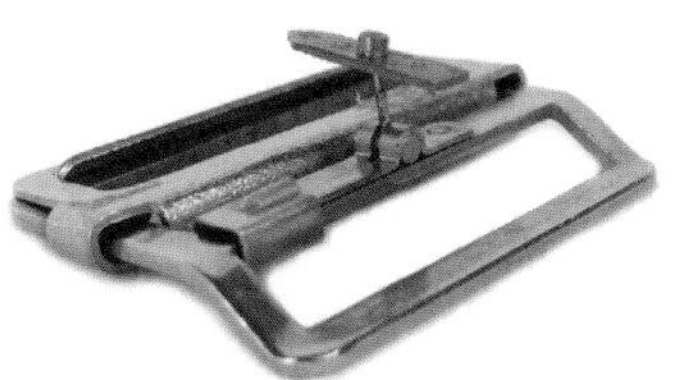

WW II RAF escape compass concealed in the buckle of a War Service Dress blouse (Suits, Aircrew). Complete and in good working order.
SOLD for
$239 / £160 / €217

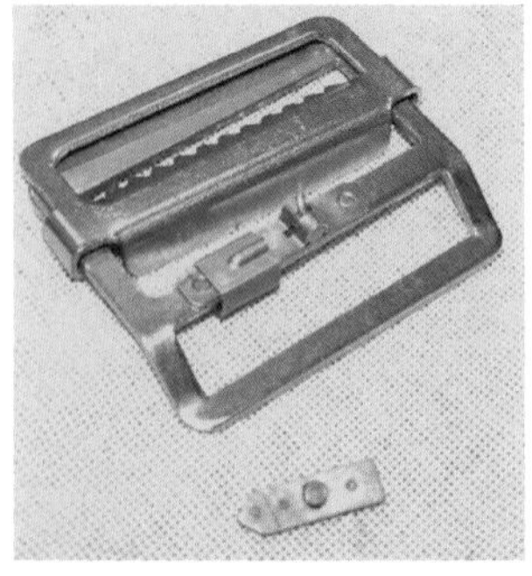

A similar item: WW II RAF escape compass concealed in the buckle of a War Service Dress blouse (Suits, Aircrew). Complete and in good working order.
**SOLD for**
**$208 / £140 / €190**

WW II RAF bar or "swinger" type escape compass. Often issued in pairs, these compasses were concealed in collars, lapels or the waist belt of the War Service Dress blouse. Could be suspended on thread or floated on water.
**SOLD together for**
**$90 / £60 / €82**

WW II RAF aircrew medical pack Mk I. As issued with full contents, pack unopened.
**SOLD for**
**$291 / £ 195 / €265**

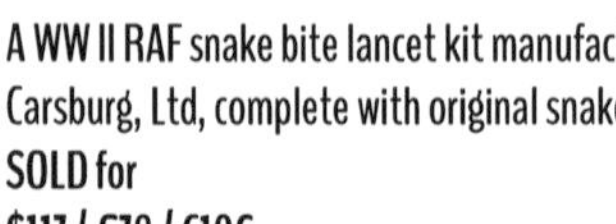

A WW II RAF snake bite lancet kit manufactured by George Carsburg, Ltd, complete with original snake bite phial.
**SOLD for**
**$117 / £78 / €106**

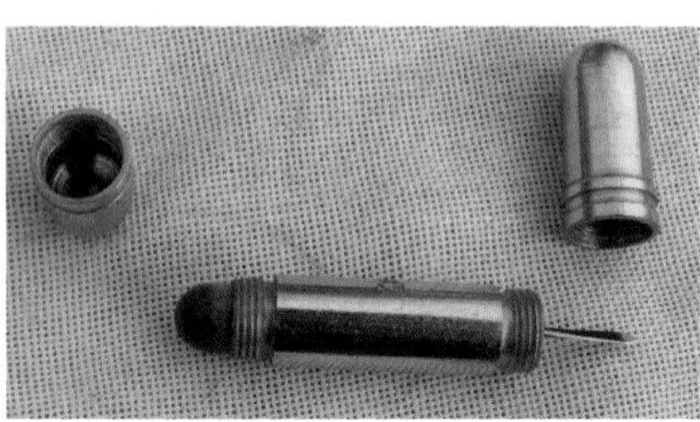

A similar RAF issue snake bite lancet kit manufactured by Gardner & Co. Ltd. London, complete with original snake bite phial.
**SOLD for**
**$112 /£75 / €102**

WW II RAF / SOE silk flag "Ghoolie" or "Blood" chit for the India / Asia Theatre, approx. 29 x 40 cm. First style printed in red and blue ink only. First style printed in red and blue ink only. Union flag and wording in 17 languages stating the owner to be an allied fighter only wanting to harm the Japanese. Stained and worn / torn in places so only fair condition.
**SOLD for**
**$75 / £48 / €60**

A similar item: WW II RAF / SOE silk flag "Ghoolie" or "Blood" chit for the India / Asia Theatre. First style printed in red and blue ink with message in 17 languages. This example in excellent condition.
**SOLD for**
**$194 / £130/ €177**

WW II RAF / SOE silk flag "Ghoolie" or "Blood" chit for the India / Asia Theatre. Second style printed in red, blue and black ink, thought to be easier to read, on rayon. Message in 17 languages with the Union flag in the upper left corner.
**SOLD for**
**$187 / £125 / €170**

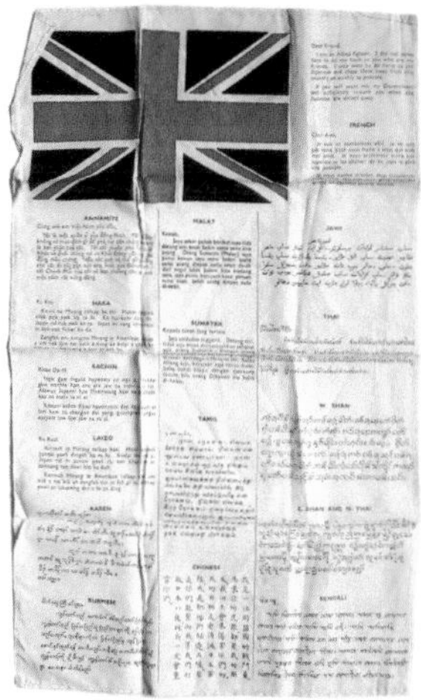

WW II RAF escape boot knife. A simple folding penknife which slipped into a pocket inside the 1943 pattern flying boots. Used for cutting away the tops of the boots, leaving what looked like ordinary civilian shoes.
**SOLD for**
**$399 / £255 / €320**

A similar RAF escape boot knife for the 1943 pattern escape boots. Excellent condition.
**SOLD for**
**$485 / £325 / €441**

A similar RAF escape boot knife for the 1943 escape pattern flying boots, but this example manufactured in stainless steel. Perhaps an early model? Faint inscription on one side.
**SOLD for**
**$359 / £240 / €340**

WW II RAF large aircrew knife carried in the Beadon Suit and survival kits. 120 mm closed. 90% of original blueing, undamaged and unsharpened. Marked AM with the Crown and G.I. & Co 22P/11
**SOLD for**
**$180 / £120 / €170**

RAF wartime dated Very Pistol cartridge tin as issued with the K dinghy packs.
**SOLD for**
**$82 / £55 / €75**

2 RAF wartime dated Very Pistol cartridge tins for red and green cartridges, no contents.
**SOLD together for**
**$75 / £50 / €68**

3 RAF wartime dated flare cartridge tins for red, green and yellow flares, lacking contents.
**SOLD together for**
**$75 / £50 / €68**

WW II RAF floating rescue lamp as issued for use with the 1941 pattern life vest. In excellent condition with wiring intact.
**SOLD for**
**$85 / £58 / €79**

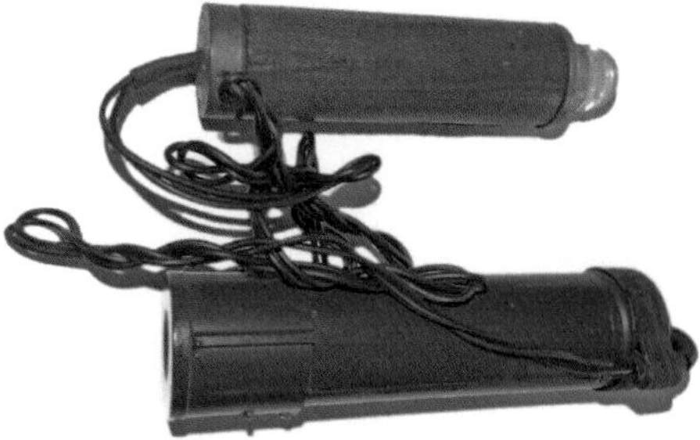

WW II RAF floating lamp in near perfect undamaged condition. Battery housing retains all original paint with AM stamp and a working bulb is in place beneath the domed lens. Actually works when batteries are fitted!
**SOLD for**
**$156 / £105 / €144**

RAF heliograph as issued with the 1941 pattern life vest and in survival kits, complete in original cloth issue case with sighting tool.
**SOLD for**
**$111 / £74 / €100**

WW II RAF K Type Dinghy. 22C/1927. Late war dinghy is in very good condition. The rubber is supple and retains all the original colour and appearance. It inflates and holds air well. Protective skirt fitted at both ends and multi-lingual instructions printed around the edges. Sea anchor and drogue are in place as is the rare CO2 bottle dated 4.43.
**SOLD for**
**$932 / £625 / €850**

WW II RAF K Type Dinghy sail. 27C/2085. Cotton fabric, dyed red and printed with sailing instructions. Good condition, retaining steering lines.
SOLD for
$115 / £75 / €101

WW II RAF K Type Dinghy mast. 27C/2054. Seven light alloy metal tubes, 38 cm folded and 1.69 m extended. Shows use and wear. Guy lines in place but fittings corroded.
SOLD for
$118 / £80 / €110

WW II RAF K Type Dinghy thwart. 27C/2057. Two pieces of plywood which lock together to hold the mast in place. Good condition with corrosion to metal parts.
SOLD for
$110 / £75 / €104

WW II RAF ration tin carried in K Dinghy pack. Stores reference 27P/7, dated 11/43 with approximately 90% of contents and instructions.
SOLD for
$299 / £200 / €272

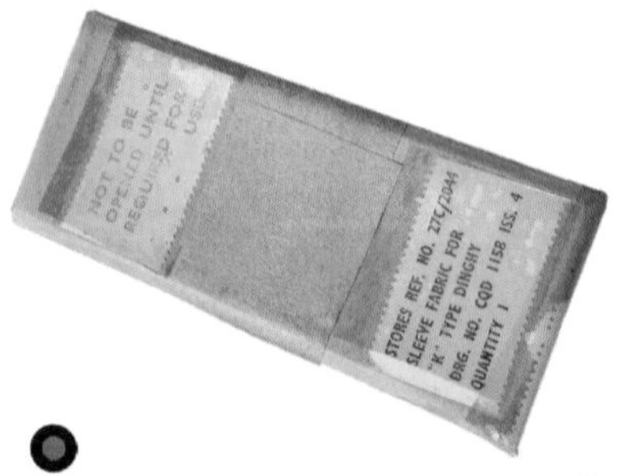


WW II RAF K Type Dinghy sleeve fabric. 27C/2044. Orange canvas sleeve approx. 27 x 10 cm used to contain the CO2 inflation cylinder, unissued in original box.
SOLD for
$37 / £25 / €35

WW II RAF K Type dinghy quick release unit. 27C/2157. Attaches to life vest and dinghy pack, enabling detachment once dinghy is deployed. Excellent used condition.
SOLD for
$52 / £35 / €48

WW II RAF Dinghy Kite. In its original packing sleeve, but without the tubular steel container. Shows little sign of use but does have one small repair. Kite suspended the aerial for "Gibson Girl" transmitter.
SOLD for
$85 / £60 / €79

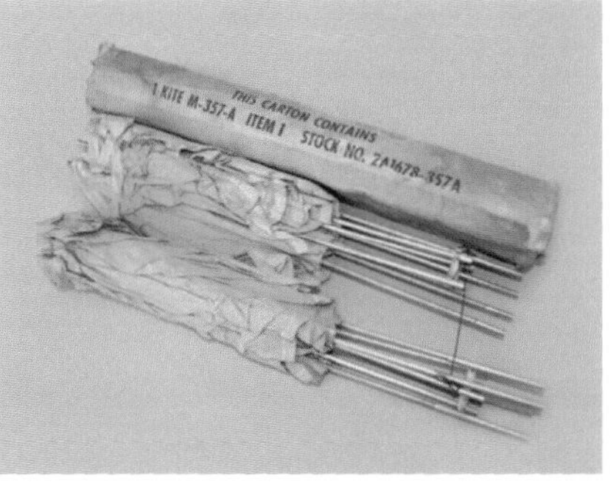


WW II RAF "Walter" Dinghy Homing Beacon (Transmitter Type T-3180) was used in the type K, Q and S dinghies. A self-contained unit comprising a battery in waterproof case, aerial mast and a small oscillator/aerial unit.
SOLD for
$475 / £325 / €450

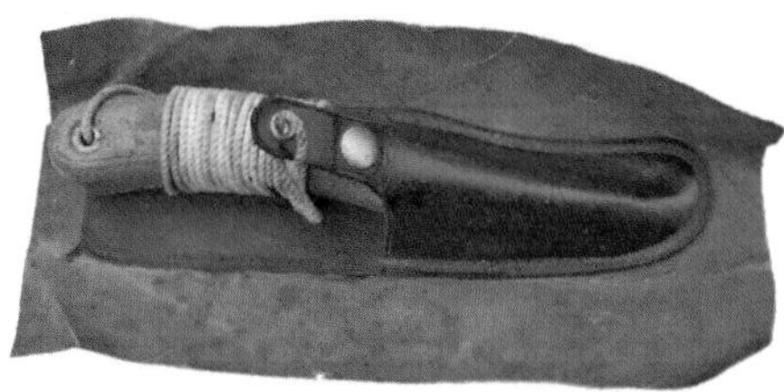

WW II RAF floating dinghy knife. 27C/2023. Issued with survival dinghies for cutting the dingy tether from a sinking aircraft, parachute pack etc. Usually glued to the side of the dinghy or pack. Curved stainless steel blade with rounded end avoids puncturing the dinghy. Blade near perfect.
SOLD for
$88 / £60 / €83

WW II RAF Dinghy seat pack Type A Mark 3* for the Type K dinghy. Stores ref. 27C/2445. Sold together with the water seat cushion, 27C/2134. The pack replaced the padded seat cushion on seat type parachutes so that pilots of single seat aircraft had a dinghy attached to them in the event of bail out over water. The cushion was used for storing fresh drinking water.
SOLD together for
$352 / £240 / €332

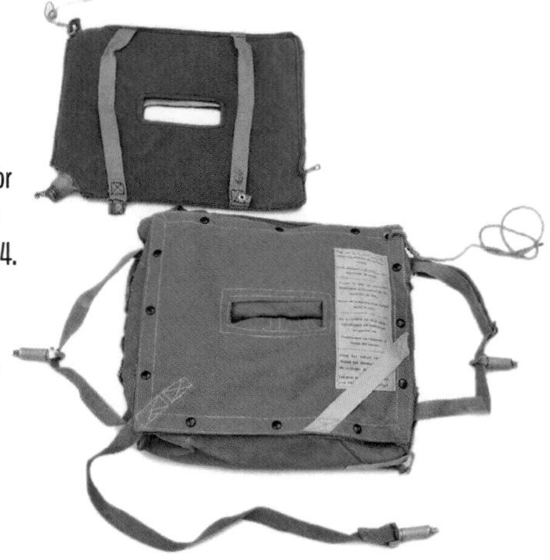

Luftwaffe Armbandkompass, 1st. Pattern, AK39 Fl 23235. Issued to all members of aircrew as an essential survival aid, this example is in good working order. Straps are original and in very good condition. The reverse shows the various markings but the second descriptive line has been erased, probably for security reasons.

**SOLD for**
**$223 / £150 / €204**

Luftwaffe Armbandkompass, AK 39 Fl 23235-1. This was the second pattern, with a high visibility face. Complete with original straps and working well. No damage apart from a very small area of white missing from the rotating rear window.

**SOLD for**
**$178 / £120 / €164**

Two inert (empty) German flare cartridges for the Luftwaffe Leuchpistole. One blue, one red, both are in good condition with surface scratching and minor dents. Markings are worn but 1944 dates are clearly visible. Very good display items.

**SOLD for**
**$75 / £50 / €69**

Bakelite Container for the Leuchpistole. A very good example of these now quite hard to find Bakelite containers for the cartridges for German flare pistols. Holds 6 cartridges, with the sixth round inverted, with a screw top making a watertight fit. Condition is very good, with no damage of any kind. Inside of the lid is marked with the manufacturer's code boa.

**SOLD for**
**$223 / £150 / €204**

Luftwaffe aircraft drinking water flask. An oversized 10 litre Luftwaffe water carrier or Trinkwasser Flasche. Although in use by all German armed forces, this example is well marked to the Luftwaffe on the base, and was carried in multi crew aircraft. Formed from a single piece of aluminium to reduce weight, the flask has a carrying handle and hinged closure lid. Overall condition is very good, with perhaps 90% paint remaining.

**SOLD for**
**$178 / £120 / €164**

Luftwaffe A2 one man life raft, Einmannschlauchboot. Complete with CO2 inflation bottle dated 20.3.44. Reputed to have been recovered by a member of the Home Guard in North London. Grubby and with several repairs, the rubber is still pliable and the raft still inflates, though the valve requires minor repairs. Sea anchor / ballast bag remains in place.

**SOLD for**
**$705 / £475 / €648**

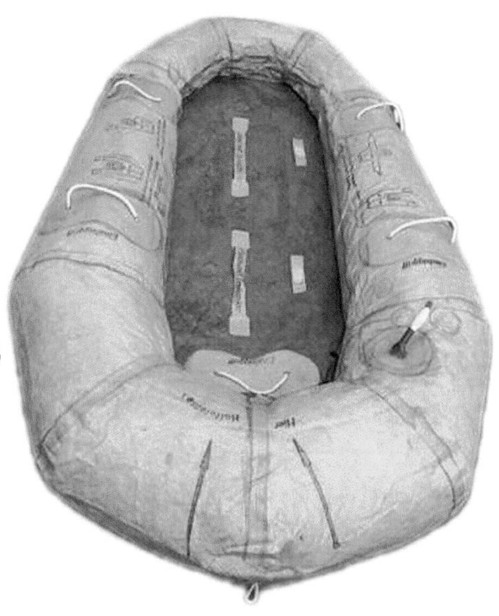

WW II Luftwaffe Seenotleucht – floating light carried by pilots and aircrews in the pocket of their Channel trousers. This example in only fair condition, but retaining partial instruction decal. Bakelite upper portion good but lower metal casing showing severe corrosion. Plastic dome and wire lanyard with clip still present.

**SOLD for**
**$510 / £345 / €479**

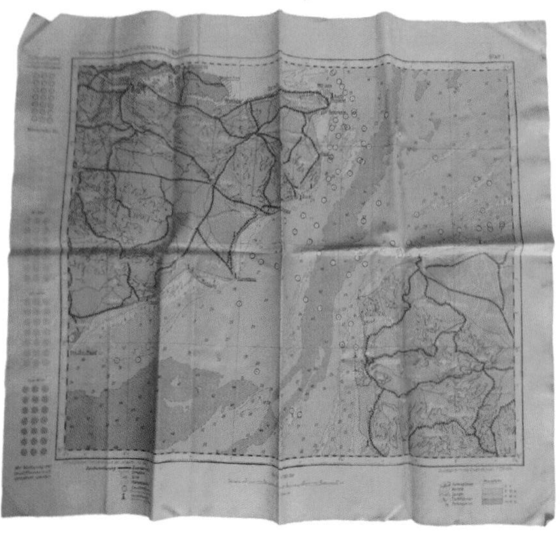

WW II Luftwaffe Küstenachtkarte (night coastal chart) of Southeast England, the Channel and Northwestern France. Used for navigation and evasion / survival. Includes Channel depths, lightships and other hazards as well as coastal towns and cities, railway lines, roads etc. 64 mm x 56 mm single sided, printed on rubberized canvas. Very good condition.
**SOLD for**
**$400 / £272 / €379**

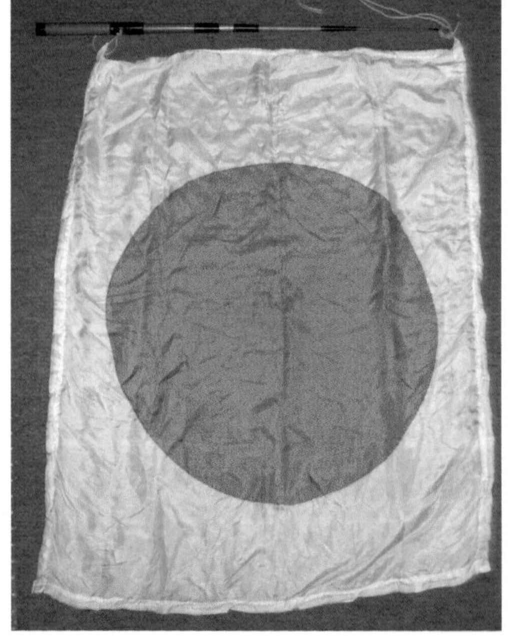

WW II Imperial Japanese bail-out / survival floating flag. The flag is silk with a buoyant material sewn into the edges. The flag is attached to its original telescoping bamboo pole and is in excellent condition. This flag would have been used as a flotation device for pilots and crews of downed aircraft.
**SOLD for**
**$365 / £250 / €345**

# WINGS / BADGES / INSIGNIA

Qualification wings
Patches
Rank badges

WW I USN pilot wing. Beautiful detailed wing with lovely patina and wear.
**SOLD for**
**$1250 / £845 / €1773**

USN cap wing by Robbins, circa 1920s.
**SOLD for**
**$ 145 / £98 / €137**

USN pilot wing from the early 1930s in Art Deco style. Gold bullion with built-up shoulders and rope detailing.
**SOLD for**
**$300 / £203 / €281**

EXTREMELY RARE CNAC (Chinese National Aviation Corporation) flight engineer shirt size wing from the World War II era. It looks identical to the pilot's wing at first glance, but has one tiny, yet very important difference. The central shield has only two characters instead of three. This is a very subtle, but very important difference between a pilot and flight engineer. This is the most rare of CNAC wings. CNAC was an airline co-owned equally by Pan Am Airlines and the Chinese government. CNAC ran many missions for the American Volunteer Group (AVG) during the war, and many AVG members became CNAC employees after the AVG disbanded.
**SOLD for**
**$2600 / £1759 / €2440**

WW II AAF bombaimer wing by Amcraft. Full size, sterling marked, pin back.
**SOLD for**
**$ 101 / £68 / €95**

WW II AAF air gunner wing by Gemsco. Two piece construction, sterling pin back.
**SOLD for**
**$ 140 / £95 / €132**

WW II AAF navigator wing made in the United Kingdom. Silver bullion wire embroidered on a blue wool background.
**SOLD for**
**$240 / £163 / €225**

WW II US Navy aircrew wing in miniature with "clutch" type pins. Sterling.
**SOLD for**
**$60 / £40 / €56**

A scarce WW II US Navy / USMC pilot wing embroidered in silver and gold bullion on green wool.
**SOLD for**
**$267 / £180 / €250**

WW II engraved Women Airforce Service Pilots (WASP) pilot wing in sterling by Josten. Dated May 20, 1944 just three days before the actual class 44-4 graduation.
**SOLD for**
**$2000 / £1353 / €1877**

WW II Women Airforce Service Pilots (WASP) uniform collar insignia in gilt with "clutch" type fasteners.
**SOLD for**
**$675 / £457 / €634**

WW II AAF rank bars (Second Lieutenant). A matching pair in leather for attaching to the epaulettes / shoulder straps on the A-2 and B-3 jacket.
**SOLD for**
**$22 / £15 / €21**

Complete set of Australian made 3rd bomb group patches, including 5th Air Force, 3rd Bomb Group, 8th Bomb Squadron, 13th Bomb Squadron (reaping skeleton), 89th Bomb Squadron and the 90th Bomb Squadron. All embroidered on felt and in excellent, unused condition.
**SOLD** as a set for
**$2980 / £2016 / €2796**

WW I RFC sweetheart wing in 15 carat gold made by Charles Packer & Co. A beautiful item.
**SOLD for**
**$267 / £180 / €250**

WW II RAF early wartime padded pilot wing brevet.
**SOLD for**
**$104 / £70 / €98**

WW II RAF heavily padded pilot wing with snaps sewn to rear for use on tropical uniform.
**SOLD for**
**$111 / £75 / €105**

WW II RAF heavily padded pilot wing brevet.
SOLD for
$89 / £60 / €83

WW II RAF flat, unpadded wings of the type found on the war service dress blouse.
SOLD for
$67 / £45 / €63

WW II RAF flat embroidered observer "half wing" brevet.
SOLD for
$60 / £40 / €56

WW II RAF flat embroidered bombaimer "half wing" brevet.
SOLD for
$52 / £35 / €49

WW II RCAF heavily padded pilot wing brevet.
SOLD for
$72 / £48 / €67

WW II RAAF flat embroidered pilot wing brevet.
SOLD for
$85 / £57/ €79

WW II RAAF flat embroidered air gunner "half wing" brevet.
SOLD for
$45 / £30 / €42

WW II RAF shoulder patch worn by American fighter pilots who flew with the Eagle Squadrons which became operational immediately following the Battle of Britain. This example is documented as having belonged to a pilot with 71 squadron, the first of the RAF Eagle Squadrons.
SOLD for
$425 / £283 / €397

WW II RAF Air Sea Rescue (ASR) service sleeve insignia. Embroidered version in excellent used condition.
SOLD for
$97 / £65 / €90

WW II RAF shoulder eagles. A matched pair in excellent condition, removed from a uniform.
SOLD for
$38 / £25 / €35

WW II RAF Warrant Officer's sleeve rank insignia. Matched pair embroidered on dark blue wool.
SOLD for
$97 / £25 / €90

WW II RAF Flight Lieutenant's shoulder boards for the greatcoat. A good quality pair, tailor made rather than issue.
SOLD for
$37 / £25 / €35

WW II RAF officer's cap badge with nice patina. Removed from cap.
SOLD for
$67 / £45 / €63

WW II South African Air Force cap badge in bronze. Eagle on a wreath surmounted by the crown with the initials in both English and Dutch.
SOLD for
$20 / £14 / €19

WW II South African Air Force officer's collar device in gilt. The same design as the cap badge but slightly smaller. A single badge (usually issued in pairs).
SOLD for
$20 / £14 / €19

WW II South African Air Force shoulder badge in bronze. The initials SAAF (English) and SALM (Dutch).
SOLD for
$20 / £14 / €19

WW II Czechoslovakia pilot badge in miniature. Though not technically authorized, these were often worn on the uniform lapel of Czech pilots serving with the RAF.
SOLD for
$104 / £70 / €98

WW II RAF Caterpillar Club grouping to a Spitfire pilot. Includes the club badge, missing one of its "ruby" eyes but properly engraved, plus a named Type C flying helmet, named parachute bag, some photographs of the award recipient and photocopy pages from his log book. Caterpillar badges to fighter pilots are quite rare.

**SOLD for**
**$1300 / £848 / €1147**

WW II RAF "winged boot" badge as awarded (unofficially) to members of the "Late Arrivals" club (pilots and aircrew who ditched, force landed or bailed out during combat, thus delaying their return back to their units). Silver boot is marked 925 on back and has 2 lugs.

**SOLD for**
**$350 / £225 / €313**

WW II RAF GQ parachute club survivor's badge. MUCH rarer than the Irvin Caterpillar pin – this beautiful winged parachute badge is made of gold, hallmarked and engraved in intricate detail to the reverse, including the phrase "GQ Parachute saved my life". Given together with an impressive certificate (see page 134). Gregory-Quilter was a relatively small contract supplier of parachutes, so few of these were presented (this is number 179 and is dated December 1943). Sadly this badge was awarded posthumously; the recipient survived his bail out only to be shot down again a few weeks later.

**SOLD for**
**$950 / £620 / €845**

WW II Luftwaffe pilot's badge and document grouping, identified to a pilot who served during the Battle of Britain with KG76, later flying the Mistel conjoined fighter / bomber aircraft. Includes several photos, Wehrpass, Iron Cross with document, cased pilot's badge with document and extensive research material.
**SOLD for**
**$1250 / £810 / €1125**

WW II German NSFK (National Socialist Flieger Korps) uniform badge. Worn on the blue grey uniform, the bevo weave insignia represents Icarus.
**SOLD for**
**$136 / £90 / €125**

WW I Italian Air Force pilot wing. Highly detailed gilt eagle and crown. Also worn by US Air Service and US Navy pilots trained in Italy in 1917-18.
**SOLD for**
**$1110 / £739 / €1035**

WW II Japanese Army Air Force pilot wing. Fine wire embroidered wing on a blue wool background with a small gilt star in the center.
**SOLD for**
**$195 / £130 / €182**

WW II Japanese Army Air Force pilot wing. Hand stitched multi-piece, woven wool on paper backing. A scarce late war example.
**SOLD for**
**$165 / £110 / €154**

WW II Japanese Army Air Force reconnaissance pilot's badge. Embroidered on a green wool background.
**SOLD for**
**$120 / £80 / €112**

WW II Japanese Army Air Force NCO pilot's graduation badge. Well worn and with a period repair to stabilize the star, nonetheless a very rare badge.
**SOLD for**
**$2300 / £1530 / €2145**

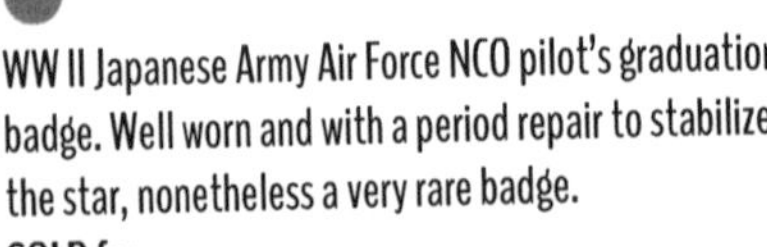

WW II Japanese Navy aviator 2nd Class badge, awarded only to naval personnel of enlisted rank who finished first in their class at flight school (there was no equivalent for officers, the 1st class version of this badge was for Petty Officers). Early bronze badge (later examples were painted brown) with gold wash on the anchor and cherry blossom.
**SOLD for**
**$695 / £463 / €649**

# AIRCRAFT PARTS & RELICS

Control grips and wheels
Aircraft parts and insignia
Cockpit instruments and switches

WW II USAAF fighter aircraft antenna radio mast. A particularly nice example, untouched since coming out of service. No data marks but research indicates it to be a model AN-104-A of the type fitted to the P-51 Mustang.

**SOLD for**
**\$112 / £75 / €104**

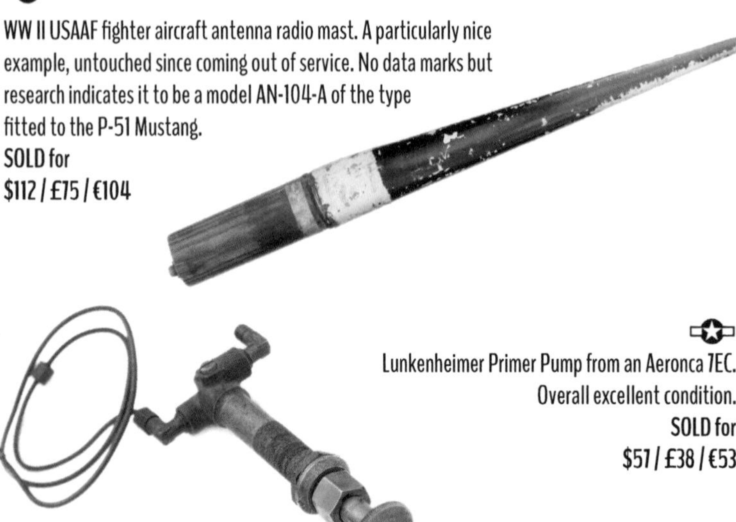

Lunkenheimer Primer Pump from an Aeronca 7EC. Overall excellent condition.

**SOLD for**
**\$57 / £38 / €53**

Control wheel from the famed Douglas C-47 Dakota troop transport aircraft which saw so much active combat in WW II and continued in USAF service through to the Vietnam war. One of the most sought after aircraft control wheels in overall excellent condition.

**SOLD for**
**\$735 / £495 / €682**

Control wheel from a RAF Canberra / USAF Martin B-57 still packed in its original box. Unissued and complete with wiring loom and all switches. Evidence of repair / resin filling around the switch module. Packing box has some distress with three corners split.

**SOLD for**
**\$245 / £165 / €228**

The LeBaudy Airship was bought for the War Office by a fund organized by the Morning Post and wrecked during a display at Farnborough on May 4th 1911, on just its second flight. Samuel Cody and Mr. de Havilland circled the airship as it began its descent, but its speed was too great and it hit trees, piercing the gas envelope and causing the crash. This 5 cm x 4 cm piece of fabric was cut from the wreckage, printed with details of the crash and sold as a souvenir.

**SOLD for**
**$39 / £25 / €35**

Memento of
Lebaudy Airship.
Wrecked at Farnboro'
May 4th, 1911.

Original Wing Strut (with Avro Transfer) believed ex-Squadron Commander's Avro 504.

**SOLD for**
**$230 / £150 / €206**

Doped canvas registration panel from De Havilland Hornet Moth c.1936, removed during restoration after a crash landing in 2001.
129" x 38" ( 328 x 97 cm).

**SOLD for**
**$107 / £70 / €96**

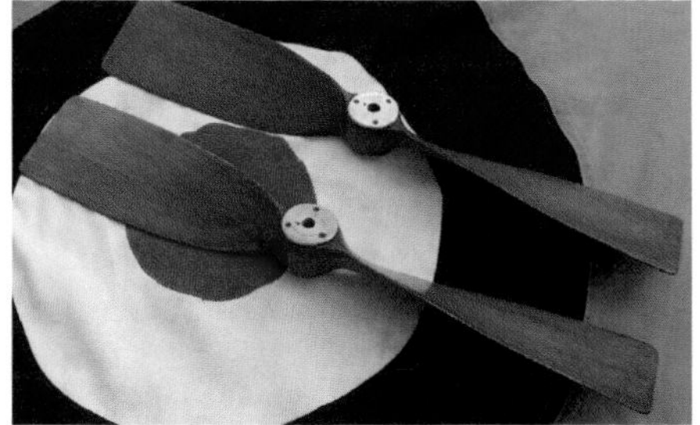

Matched set of aircraft wind generator propellers c.1920s, 21" diameter.

**SOLD as a pair for**
**$421 / £275 / €378**

Pair of RAF aircraft roundels painted on original doped canvas, c.1920s.
**SOLD** as a pair for
$ 390 / £250 / €350

Painted panel from an RAF aircraft featuring the badge of 13 Squadron. Canvas on wood frame.
**SOLD for**
$130 / £85 / €117

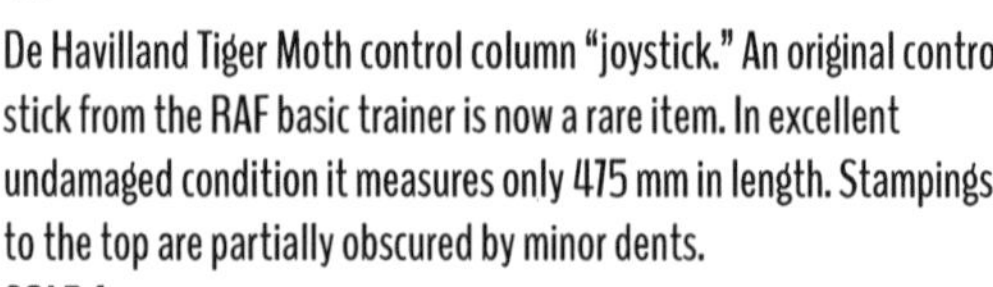

De Havilland Tiger Moth control column "joystick." An original control stick from the RAF basic trainer is now a rare item. In excellent undamaged condition it measures only 475 mm in length. Stampings to the top are partially obscured by minor dents.
**SOLD for**
$223 / £150 / €207

Control column top / half-wheel as fitted to the Bristol Blenheim Mk I or Mk IV and Bristol Beaufighter. Fitted with the guts of the machine gun-firing mechanism (lacking firing button). Excellent condition overall, may have been re-coated. Visible serial number.
**SOLD for**
$950 / £605 / €765

Control column ring or "spade" grip from a Supermarine Spitfire, probably a Mk IB or IIB. Fitted with early cannon firing button and camera-gun button (replacement). Retains good brake lever and 75% of original Dunlop rubber coating. Top of chain housing still attached. Moving parts are frozen, magnesium alloy handle is corroded and semi-relic condition.

**SOLD for**
**$1928 / £1300 / €1790**

RAF Hawker Typhoon / Tempest Spade Grip. An extremely rare unrestored control column grip, model AH8005, as fitted to Typhoon and Tempest fighters. The electric firing button is fully operable. Hard rubber covering is original and unrestored, with minor cracking and shrinkage on the upper right. Brake lever is a reproduction but an original camera gun button is included.

**SOLD for**
**$1930 / £1300 / €1791**

RAF Control column spade grip AH8090. This type was used in the Meteor I, III and IV, Spitfire Mk 22 and Tempest II, IV and VI but this most probably came from an early Meteor. Standard ring or spade grip with part rubber and part cord binding wrap and "Selectric" gun button plus an early push-to-talk switch. Original brake lever works fine as do all the other buttons and features.

**SOLD for**
**$1750 / £1115 / €1415**

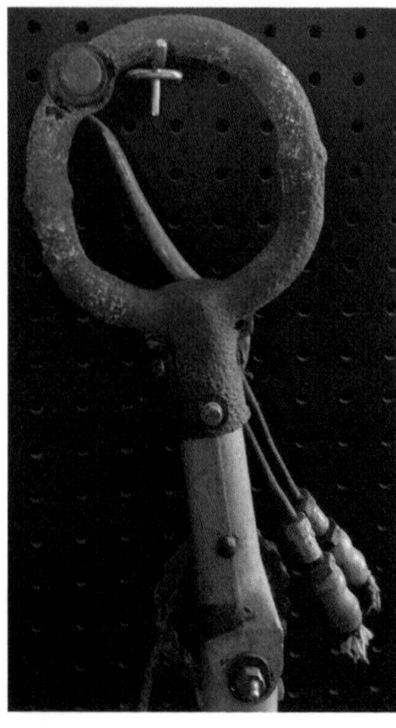

Complete Hurricane control column and spade grip from a Hawker Hurricane Mk IIB with known history and provenance. In "as found" condition salvaged from a crash site in Russia. This aircraft served in the RAF before being shipped to the Soviet Union. It was shot down in October 1942 and salvaged from a swamp near the Finnish border in 1997. Includes the spade or ring grip, brake lever and part of the brake cable, pneumatic pipes, chain cog and part of the chain (seen on the back, frozen in place) as well as the full control column and the connecting rod for the elevators

**SOLD for**
**$2500 / £1630 / €2240**

RAF control column spade grip AH8400. This smaller "half" spade design was fitted to the Sea Fury, later Spitfires (F22 and 24), Vampire and Meteor. In excellent condition with functioning "Selectric" gun button and brake lever. Original black painted finish.

**SOLD for**
**$1170 / £850 / €1260**

Control stick top from a RAF Meteor T7. Type of stick used on early jets, prior to the use of ejector seats (the ring grip could cause injury during ejection). Switches work and original brake lever is still in place. Loss of paint to the lower tubular fixing which also shows a clear stamp AH9365. Covering has become loose but present.

**SOLD for**
**$571 / £385 / €531**

Hawker Hurricane tailwheel. Identified as being from a Mk II Hurricane and bearing the part number AHO 5048, the wheel and tyre display have been mounted on a nicely crafted wooden stand. Wheel and tyre in fair condition only, the reverse showing some corrosion, age and cracking with loss to the exterior rubber revealing the cord.
SOLD for
$193 / £130 / €180

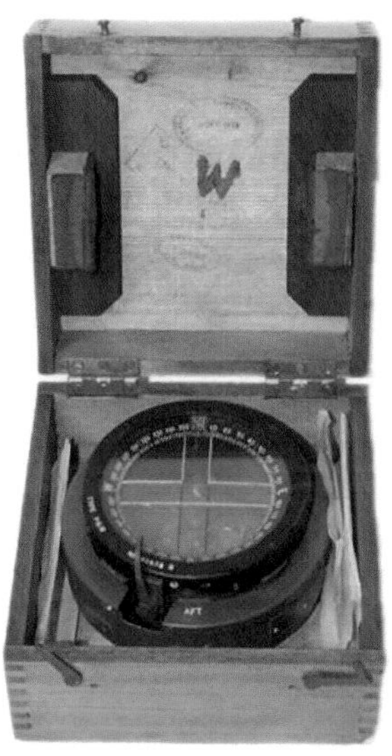


WW II RAF P 8 magnetic compass in wooden transit case. Fitted to such aircraft as the Spitfire, Hurricane and Tiger Moth, amongst others. In excellent condition with prominent A.M. markings and stores reference number 6A/0726. In good working order, however, there is no damping fluid inside and this has resulted in some flaking to the background black paint. The case has inspection dates from Sept 1939 to Nov 1943 and includes two envelopes, one with spare screws, the other containing optical tubes.
SOLD for
$127 / £85 / €118

Liquid filled compass from a WW II Royal Navy Fleet Air Arm Fairey Swordfish. Overall good condition with minor paint loss, retaining 80% original fluid.
SOLD for
$99 / £64 / €80

Lancaster Bomb Release Switchbox, Type F. Bomb selector switchbox used in the Lancaster and other heavy bombers. A.M. marked and with reference number 5D/656, in good condition but missing six small screws. All switches operate well and knob on the right hand side rotates the selector window.
**SOLD for**
**$127 / £85 / €118**

RAF Cockpit Lamp 5C/366. Unissued condition and still contained in its original packing. This is the heavy brass version – a black Bakelite version was also produced.
**SOLD for**
**$67 / £45 / €62**

Air Ministry Double Magneto Switch as fitted to the Spitfire and other RAF aircraft.
**SOLD for**
**$57 / £38 / €53**

RAF Cockpit Oxygen Connector Socket Mk IIIc as fitted to all cockpits, turrets, navigators' and bomb aimers' positions etc. Unissued condition and still with its original grease proof wrapping paper.
**SOLD for**
**$60 / £40 / €56**

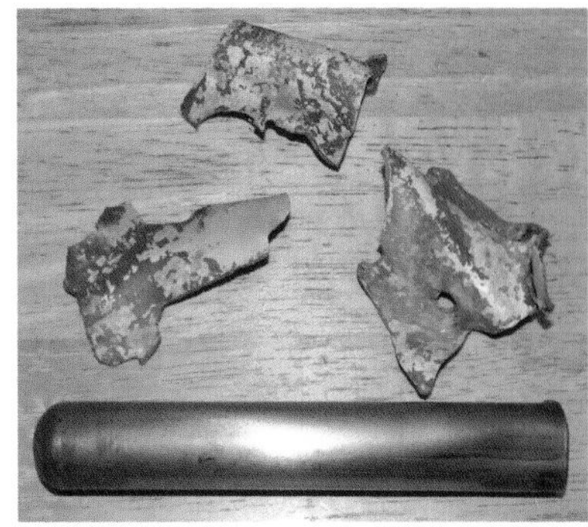

The pitot head excavated from the crash site of Al Deere's famous Battle of Britain aircraft "Kiwi2" KL-B, together with 3 small pieces of aluminium aircraft skin, retaining camouflage paint,from the same crash site.
SOLD for
$ 250 / £169 / €233

RAF aircraft rear view mirror of the type fitted to fighter aircraft such as the Spitfire, Hurricane, Tempest, Typhoon, etc. H & S. 'Mirrors, Aircraft, Type B.' Stores ref. 27H/2017. Comprises a brass domed casing with internal bracket mount point, mirrored glass and edge ring bezel. Air Ministry marks and reference numbers are stamped around the edge.
SOLD for
$668 / £450 / €621

RAF / Royal Navy throttle quadrant from a Fleet Air Arm Hawker Sea Fury circa 1950s. In good display condition. Some levers have been removed but could be easily restored.
SOLD for
$284 / £190/ €262

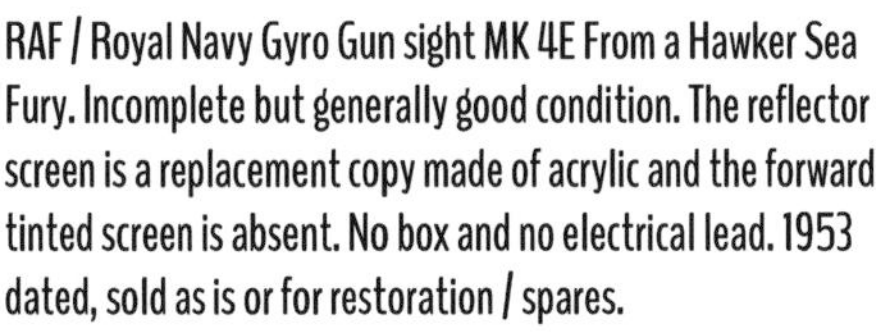

RAF / Royal Navy Gyro Gun sight MK 4E From a Hawker Sea Fury. Incomplete but generally good condition. The reflector screen is a replacement copy made of acrylic and the forward tinted screen is absent. No box and no electrical lead. 1953 dated, sold as is or for restoration / spares.
SOLD for
$127 / £85 / €117

Complete tail fin panel with swastika from a FW 190, authenticated and with researched history. Shot down over Normandy in July 1944 and shows battle damage. Unusual to find "trophies" such as this that have not been cut down for mounting or framing.
**SOLD for**
**$7500 / £5060 / €6067**

Luftwaffe LKu 4 Gyro Kompass by Siemens, model number Fl 22561. Type fitted to the instrument panel of a range of WW II Luftwaffe aircraft including Ju88, He111 and Me110.
**SOLD for**
**$241 / £162 / €224**

# AVIATION EPHEMERA

Supplementary equipment
Clocks and watches
Log books, documents and paper items
Ceremonial items
Trench art
Personal and homefront items

WW II AAF / USN airplane mooring kit Type D 1. Complete and in original storage case.
**SOLD for**
**$98 / £65 / €90**

WW II AAF Pilots Navigation Kit. Leather valise as issued to pilots, co-pilots and navigators, with pockets inside for maps and navigation equipment.
**SOLD for**
**$80 / £53 / €74**

WW II AAF aircrew lunch ration by Charms Company, Bloomfield, New Jersey. Pocket-sized box with twin compartments containing two sticks of chewing gum, two bars of fudge and 2 oz. of hard candy. Issued individually to aircrews on missions longer than three hours.
**SOLD for**
**$60 / £40 / €55**

WW II AAF Type A-3 gunner's safety belt, by Companion Bags Inc. Used mainly by waist gunners to prevent them from falling from the aircraft. Date of manufacture September 1943.
**SOLD for**
**$120 / £80 / €111**

WW II AAF A-11 "hack" wristwatch by the Bulova Watch Co. with a 1943 contract date and good AAF markings. Black dial with luminous hands and sweep second hand. 16-jewel 'hack' movement. Some minor scratching and tarnishing, dial and crystal both very good. Replacement strap. In good working order.

**SOLD for**
**$304 / £200 / €271**

WW II AAF Pilots Watch type A-12 by Elgin. Extremely rare watch, similar to the standard issue A-11 but with a 24-hour dial, for issue to B-29 pilots. Green canvas strap. Excellent working condition and marked on reverse with a serial number.

**SOLD for**
**$1200 / £796 / €1107**

WW II AAF / USN 8-day chronograph (AN 5741-1) mounted to a brass frame. Used in heavy bombers. Made by Elgin National Watch Company, the 24 hour dial has four smaller gauges for date, lapsed time, seconds, etc. In good working order.

**SOLD for**
**$400 / £265 / €370**

WW II AAF Type A-8 navigator's stopwatch by Elgin. 15 jewel stopwatch made in 1943 with a gold-flashed movement. Runs at 40 beats per second and makes a buzzing sound that gave it the nickname "Jitterbug". The dial makes a smooth sweep every 10 seconds. Still in its original cardboard storage box with FRAGILE label.

**SOLD for**
**$250 / £166 / €231**

WW II AAF Aircrew flight operation/cruising guide cards for the P-51D & K Mustang. Set of 4 plastic cards with information about the aircraft's engine performance in different scenarios.

**SOLD for**
**$38 / £25 / €35**

WW II AAF Aircrew flight operation/cruising guide cards for the B-17G Flying Fortress. Similar to the cards above but a set of 8 cards for the 4-engine bomber.

**SOLD for**
**$400 / £265 / €370**

WW I 25th aero squadron trench art. Decorated shell casing from the US Army Air Service 25th Aero Squadron with an engraved likeness of the squadron's emblem, a masked, axe-yielding executioner.

**$575 / £382 / €530**

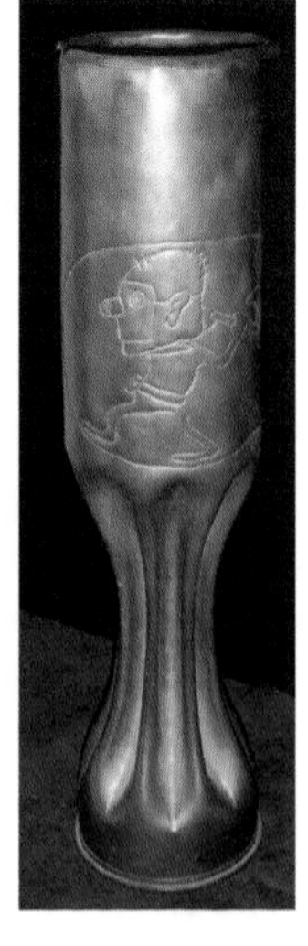

WW I US Army Air Service clock from Kelly Field, San Antonio, Texas. The clock is mounted inside the copper tip of a WW I wooden aircraft propeller mounted to a hand-painted, oval wooden base.

**SOLD for**
**$350 / £233 / €323**

WW I RFC message streamer. Brightly coloured fabric streamer with a compartment for inserting a message, weighted at one end. Thrown from aircraft to commanders "in the field" with message / orders from HQ.
SOLD for
$56/ £31 / €52

WW I RFC Map Board Mk 1. Manufactured by The General Instrument and Engineering Co. Ltd, London. With spare plotting acetate.
SOLD for
$354 / £235/ €327

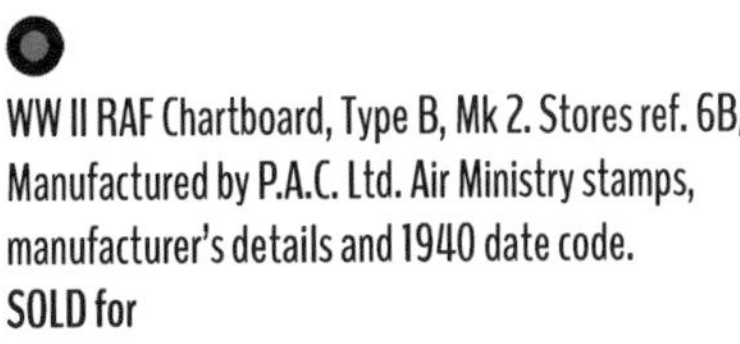

WW II RAF Chartboard, Type B, Mk 2. Stores ref. 6B/137. Manufactured by P.A.C. Ltd. Air Ministry stamps, manufacturer's details and 1940 date code.
SOLD for
$181 / £120 / €167

WW II RAF navigator's holdall. Stores ref. 1A/3927 by Waring & Gillow Ltd. Extremely rare light green canvas bag for carrying the chartboard and all instruments. War Department broad arrow marked and dated 1943.
SOLD for
$460 / £305 / €425

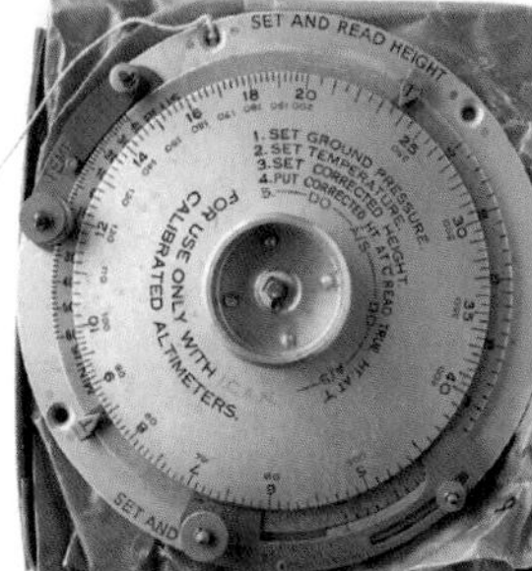


WW II RAF Height and Airspeed Computor Mk IIA. By Betta Manufacturing Company, Enfield. Stores reference 6B/166. Dated 1947.
SOLD for
$75 / £50 / €70

RAF carpenter's ruler, dated 1931. Probably used while working on wooden airfames.
**SOLD for**
**$27 / £18 / €25**

WW II RAF oil can by T.E. Bladon. The base of the spout clearly stamped with the maker's name and Air Ministry property mark together with the date 1938.
**SOLD for**
**$48 / £32 / €45**

WW II RAF Air Ministry marked aircraft tyre pressure gauge in its original leather case.
**SOLD for**
**$53 / £35 / €49**

WW II RN Fleet Air Arm Pilots flight / knee board. This example would appear to have been made by a ship's carpenter or rigger from varnished marine ply and a sheet of clear Perspex held in place by bulldog clips.
**SOLD for**
**$48 / £32 / €45**

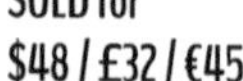

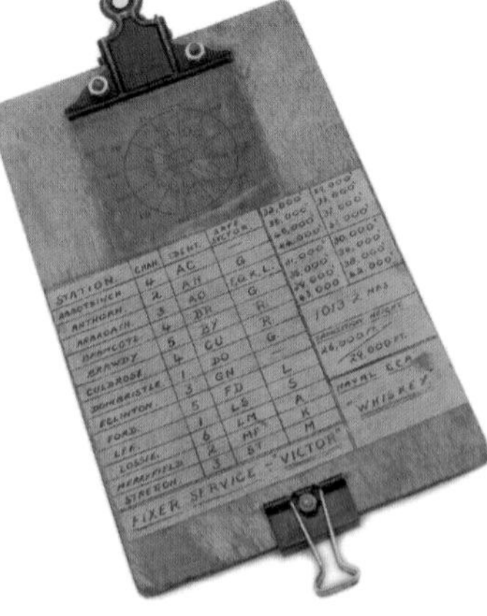

WW II RN Fleet Air Arm call signs and codes book. Two heavy cardboard covers bound together with acetate pouches and sheets for adding relevant daily codes, transmissions, etc. Also contains photographic prints of ID silhouettes of German and Japanese ships. Elastic straps enable it to be worn as a knee board while flying.
**SOLD for**
**$225 / £150 / €209**

WW II RAF Binoculars, Prismatic, 5 x 40 Mk IV. Stores ref. 6E/383. Manufactured by Ross and designed with large lenses and eye shield to improve night vision. Complete with original, hard leather case and shoulder strap.

**SOLD for**
**$166 / £110 / €153**

WW II RAF Hand held rangefinder. Made of Bakelite by Fidelity Engineering Co. Ltd. for determining range of various allied and enemy aircraft.

**SOLD for**
**$121 / £80 / €112**

WW II RAF ops room metal aircraft counters. Mounted on wooden blocks and moved across the ops room plotting table by WAAFs with croupier type rakes, indicating height and numbers of enemy aircraft. Approx. 3 x 2.5 cm.

**SOLD each for**
**$60 / £40 / €56**

WW II RAF ops room / dispersal hut telephone. Air Ministry marked and made by the Telephone Manufacturing Company in London. Handset Telephone Type 350, stores ref. 10AH/1565 and battery-less Type 61 base. Winder works well and overall condition is excellent. Original cord without wear or damage.

**SOLD for**
**$242 / £160 / €224**

WW II RAF Stereoscope 14b/746. Used for photographic interpretation, this example is in excellent condition and complete with canvas bag. Air Ministry marked, the set shows no real signs of use.
SOLD for
$68 / £45 / €63

WW II RAF observer's pocket watch. Stores ref. 6E/50. Swiss made 16-jewel movement. White dial with luminous numerals and hands plus seconds dial. Screw-back with War Department broad arrow and serial number engraved. The dial has minor marking. Replacement plastic crystal. Case has normal wear and tear but no damage.
SOLD for
$121 / £110 / €112

WW II RAF navigator's stopwatch dated 1936. Overall condition is very good with all functions working well. Air Ministry marked and with stores ref. 6B/117.
SOLD for
$106 / £70 / €98

RAF Flying Training Manual, Part 1, Flying Instruction AP129. 1934 edition with amendments up to 1935 contained in its original board covers with string ties. Manual appears complete and in very good condition with light damage to the corners of the covers. Issued to all new pilot trainees.
SOLD for
$60 / £35 / €56

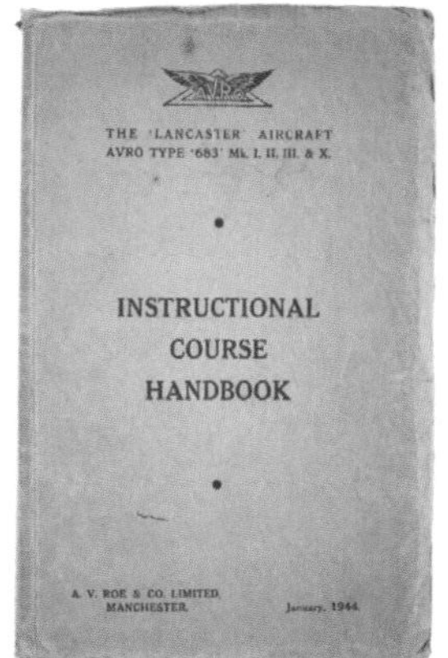


WW II RAF Instructional Course Handbook for the Lancaster aircraft, Mk. 1., II, III & X. Published by A.V. Roe & Co. Ltd., Manchester, June 1944. Card cover, 15 x 22 cm. Approx. 64p plus 20 pullout diagrams.
SOLD for
$144 / £95 / €133

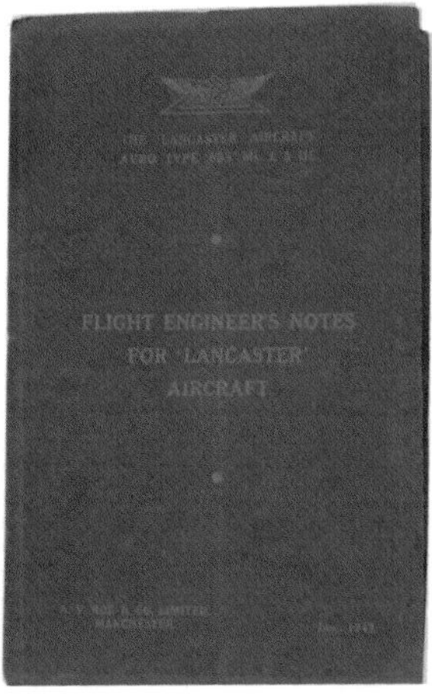

WW II RAF notes for the Lancaster (AVRO Type '683' MK. I & III). Published by A.V. Roe & Co. Ltd., Manchester, June 1943. Card covers, 15 x 23 cm. Approximately 36 pages plus around 13 pullout diagram/charts. The book covers fuel and oil systems; aeroplane controls; engine controls; handling; operating data; emergency procedures etc.
SOLD for
$153 / £100 / €137

WW II RAF observer's and air gunner's log books and miniature medals to an air gunner who served during the Battle of Britain. Log books include many notable signatures including that of Wing Commander, Guy Gibson, VC (then Flt. Lt.) who flew one tour of ops with Fighter Command in 1940-41.
SOLD for
$3480 / £2250 / €3120

WW II RAF Service dress cap and logbook to a RAF Catalina flying boat pilot. The cap can quite honestly be described as "Salty", the family recalling that it was blown into the sea on more than one occasion. The Logbook covers are faded but it is otherwise in very good condition, with 1860 hours flying time, including his wartime service on anti-submarine patrols, convoy escorts and air sea rescue.
**SOLD for**
**$620 / £400 / €555**

WW II WAAF grouping of books, documents and photographs relating to a WAAF who trained at 1 BTU (Balloon Training Unit), Cardington in Bedfordshire. Includes several books, notebooks and photographs, one in a period, Art Deco style wood and glass frame.
**SOLD for**
**$192 / £125 / €170**

WW II RAF GQ parachute club survivor's certificate, usually issued with a gold pin (see page 112). Beautifully calligraphed certificate measures 10.5 x 15.5 inches with a debossed and tipped in colour plate of a parachutist, plus gold foil / emboss GQ winged parachute emblem. The gold foil has oxidized slightly but the colour plate is still bright and vibrant. Far less of these were awarded during the war than caterpillar club cards, because Gregory-Quilter was a relatively small contract supplier.
**SOLD for**
**$750 / £489 / €667**

Whereas by virtue of your successful accomplishment of a descent from the upper airs of this planet by Parachute we have thought fit to nominate and appoint you
Sergeant R. Mitchell. R.A.F.
to be a member of the G Q Club
We do by these presents bestow upon you the dignity of membership and hereby authorize you to have hold and enjoy the privilege of wearing its gold badge of two wings
without challenge, let or hindrance
Given under our hand this day

G.Q. PARACHUTE COMPANY LTD. STADIUM WORKS, WOKING, SURREY

WW II RAF Target Map No.6 (d) (vi) 95, Railway Marshalling Yard, Stettin, Germany, dated April 1942. Scale 1:63.360. Intelligence map of the marshalling yards at Stettin. Marked with concentric rings, one mile apart, around the centre of the target. Marked in chinagraph pencil and creased, dog-eared with edge tears and a taped repair.
**SOLD for**
**$41 / £30 / €46**

WW II RAF Captains of Aircraft maps. Essentially route maps showing spot heights, borders, rivers, major cities and coastlines for pilots to follow the track planned by the navigator.
**Each SOLD individually for**
**$83 / £55 / €77**

WW II RAF map. Air sheet 9, 2nd war revision, dated 10/1944. 1/4" to 1 mile. Approx. 78 x 59 cm. Shows war-time air bases including many of the famous 8th AAF bases including Earls Colne, Sudbury, Andrews Field, Lavenham, Thorpe Abbotts, Old Buckenham, Coltishall, Downham Market, Bassingbourne, Duxford, Hornchurch, Hendon etc.
**SOLD for**
**$30 / £20 / €28**

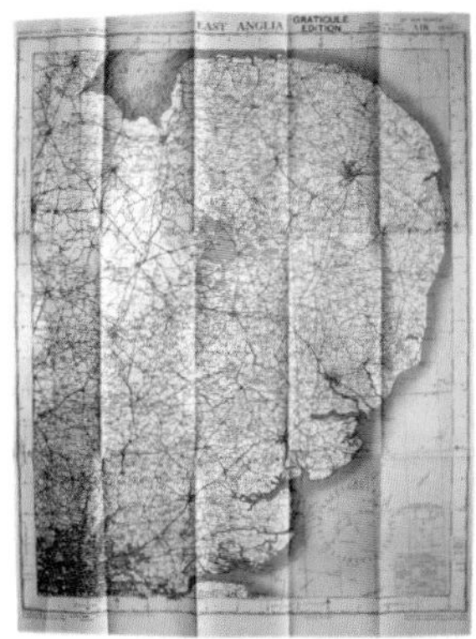

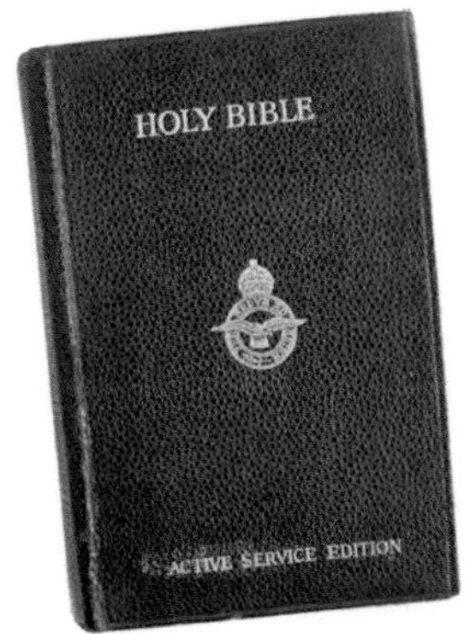


WW II RAF Holy Bible, Active Service Edition. Hard cover, 9.5 x 14 cm. Contains both old and new testaments and has a message from His Majesty The King on the frontispiece. Dated September 1939.
**SOLD for**
**$23 / £15 / €21**

WW II RAF ensign or "duster," complete with toggle and rope. Full size, wool flag sewn from sections of different colours. Broad arrow marked and date stamped 1945.
**SOLD for**
**$295 / £195 / €272**

WW II RAF Staff Car Pennant. Flown from staff cars of station commanders of the rank of Wing Commander and above.
**SOLD for**
**$103 / £68 / €95**

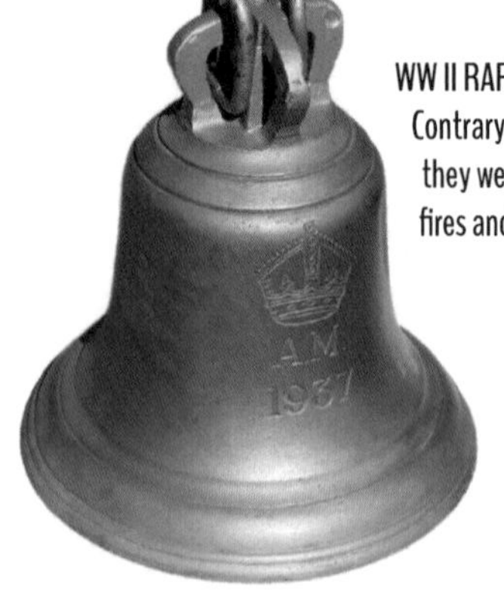


WW II RAF "scramble" bell dated 1937 with original rope and clapper. Contrary to popular myth, each station had more than one bell and they were not used exclusively to scramble aircraft! (For example, fires and other emergencies). Nonetheless an iconic symbol of RAF fighter pilots.
**SOLD for**
**$1403 / £925 / €1292**

WW II RAF "scramble" bell, dated 1940. Measuring approximately 33 cm in height and 33 cm diameter. Large nickel plated bronze RAF station bell with classic crown top. Stamped 'A.T.W.' and with War Department broad arrow on the crown top and engraved with the Air Ministry crown and date. Fitted with the original clapper and rope. In totally original unrestored condition.
**SOLD for**
**$2275 / £1500 / €2095**

A similar large size WW II RAF "scramble" bell dated 1941, retaining its nickel silver plating and original rope and clapper.
**SOLD for**
**$1896 / £1250 / €1745**

WW II RAF squadron plaque for 600 "City of London" Squadron. Formed in 1925 as a light bomber squadron, they were equipped with Blenheim aircraft and fought with distinction during the Battle of Britain.
**SOLD for**
**$42 / £28 / €40**

WW II RAF brocade table or altar cloth. Approx. 2 x 1.4 m. Very high quality heavy cotton damask fabric. Off white with a woven pattern and border. To the centre there is a large RAF King's crown crest, approx. 32 x 40 cm.
**SOLD for**
**$303 / £200 / €280**

WW II RAF "bird's claw" style sugar or ice tongs, probably from an RAF officer's mess. Marked 'GG S S' and EPNS. Approx. 15.5 cm in length.
**SOLD for**
**$91 / £60 / €84**

WW II RAF nut crackers by Walker & Hall. Approx. 13 cm in length. Marked EPNS and RAF King's crown crest to handle. 1936 date code.
**SOLD for**
**$68 / £45 / €63**

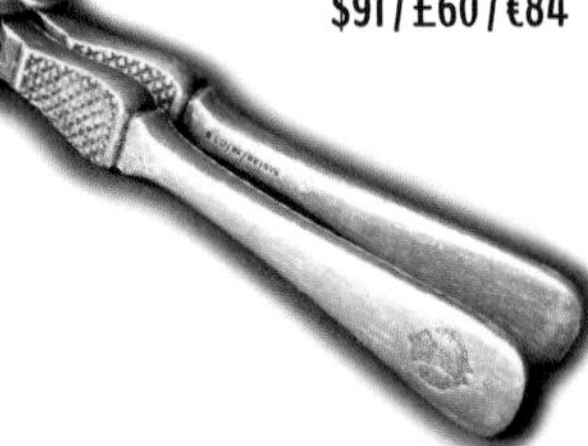

WW I trench art tobacco barrel from 60 Squadron, Royal Flying Corps. Made from the propeller hub of one of the squadron's SE5A aircraft. Engraved 'No 60 Squadron' with the image of an SE5A below. Sold with full provenance.
**SOLD for**
**\$303 / £200 / €279**

WW I trench art made from a Royal Flying Corps aircraft propeller blade with aneroid barometer mounted to centre. 39" (99 cm) in height.
**SOLD for**
**\$144 / £95 / €133**

WW I RFC trench art shell case. To one side an image of the Royal Flying Corps cipher with a crown and laurel leaves. To the other side, a crudely engraved four bladed propeller with the dates 1912-18 below.
**SOLD for**
**\$33 / £22 / €31**

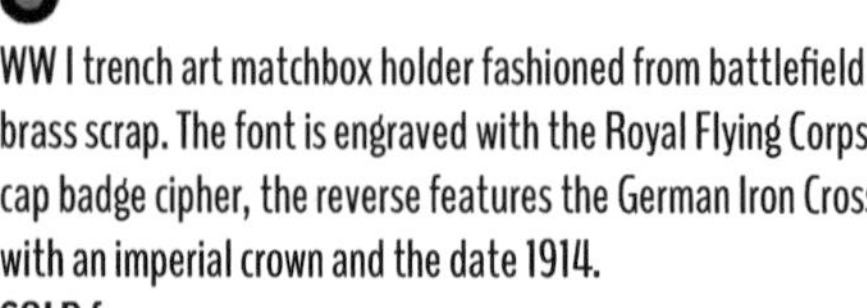

WW I trench art matchbox holder fashioned from battlefield brass scrap. The font is engraved with the Royal Flying Corps cap badge cipher, the reverse features the German Iron Cross with an imperial crown and the date 1914.
**SOLD for**
**\$33 / £22 / €31**

WW I Royal Flying Corps cigarette case made from solid silver and finely engraved with the RFC pilot wing, with France, Egypt, Salonica and Macedonia followed by the dates 1916-17-18 and final campaigns listed as Malta, Crete and Italy.
SOLD for
$295 / £195 / €272

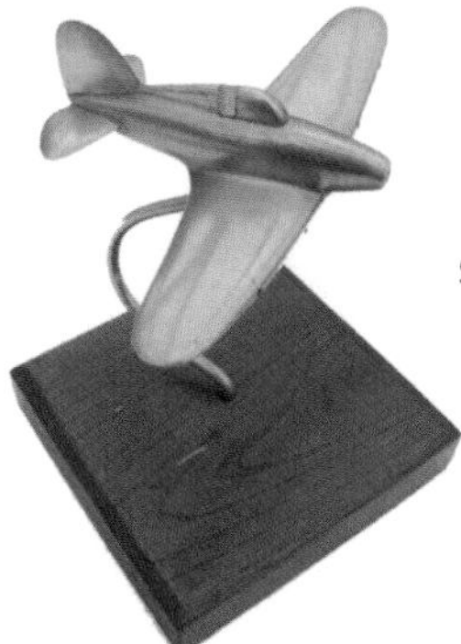

WW II trench art model aircraft. Many of these models are quite difficult to identify. This cast alloy example might be a somewhat stylized Hawker Hurricane lacking its propeller, or an early attempt at capturing the shape of Britain's first jet aircraft, the Gloster E28 / 29 "Whittle". Nonetheless, highly collectible.
SOLD for
$64 / £42 / €59

A little easier to recognize is this brass WW II trench art model of a Lockheed Hudson on a copper / bronze base.
SOLD for
$106 / £70 / €98

WW II trench art table lamp in the Art Deco style, the base and stem are all constructed of material salvaged from aircraft canopy perspex, complete with a decorative gilt RAF sweetheart pilot wing mounted to the stand.
SOLD for
$129 / £85 / €119

WW II RAF/RAAF propaganda / sweetheart scarf. Rectangular, approximately 90 x 85 cm and hemmed at the edges. Off white scarf decorated with a repeat pattern of RAAF pilot wings and a quote from Churchill's famous speech given in tribute to Battle of Britain pilots, “Never was so much owed by so many to so few.”

**SOLD for**
**$190 / £125 / €175**

Manufactured by Norah Wellings who was a chief doll designer for Chad Valley prior to establishing her own company. “Harry the Hawk” was created to raise funds during the war for the RAF Comforts Committee, with a percentage of the sale donated to the fund. Harry is an airman/pilot approximately 18 cm / 7” tall, kitted out in a Sidcot suit, flying helmet, boots, gloves and parachute harness with pack and canopy, all made of felt and velvet. The doll is soft bodied with hand painted features. Labeled ‘Made in England by Norah Wellings’ and ‘Royal Air Force Comforts Fund U.K. Regd. Design No. 837533”. Missing the felt goggles but otherwise complete.

**SOLD for**
**$266 / £175 / €244**

Air-Sea Rescue game. Sold during the war by arrangement with the RAF Benevolent Fund. Made by Raphael Tuck & Sons Ltd. Game board is printed on war economy card. Includes dice and shaker, all playing pieces and instruction leaflet in original box.

**SOLD for**
**$190 / £125 / €175**

WW II German dead reckoning computer Model DR-3, Fl. Nr. 23825-2. Manufactured by Denner & Pape of Hamburg. The DR 3 was an improved version of the DR 2 'triangle' computer commonly referred to by pilots as a Knemeyer. 15 cm in diameter with a rotating inner ring and perspex 'pointer' arms. Dated July 1943.

SOLD for
$136 / £90 / €125

WW II Luftwaffe station clock by Junghans, dated 1938. 125 mm tall. Very collectible and ideal for everyday use or display. The Junghans J30 movement runs well and keeps good time. Dial is marked with the Junghans logo and the Luftwaffe reference number FL25591.

SOLD for
$555 / £365 / €510

WW II Luftwaffe log book grouping to a radio operator with KG26, heavily involved in the Battle of France and Battle of Britain with many operational flights, bombing raids and combat. Includes his Iron Cross 2nd Class and several photographs.

SOLD for
$1315 / £850 / €1180

WW II Luftwaffe navigation chart identified to KG255 covering the whole of Germany. 1200 mm x 970 mm. 16 panels on a blue linen backing showing airfields, navigation beacons, danger areas etc. KG255 became KG51 in May 1939 and was heavily involved in the Battle of France and Battle of Britain.

SOLD for
$182 / £120 / €168

WW II Luftwaffe navigation map for single seat aircraft, or aircraft which did not carry a navigator. Map comprises four waxed panels, foil backed and affixed to card and covering the whole of Germany with its borders. Clear BAL inspection stamp and dated 8.2.40.
**SOLD for**
**$182 / £120 / €168**

WW II Luftwaffe officer's dress sword by Eickhorn. Early example with nickel silver plated fittings, all in very good condition and complete with scabbard and hanger.
**SOLD for**
**$1306 / £860 / €1201**

WW II Luftwaffe mess hall dinner plate, dated 1940. In excellent condition and perfect for a Battle of Britain display.
**SOLD for**
**$68 / £45 / €63**

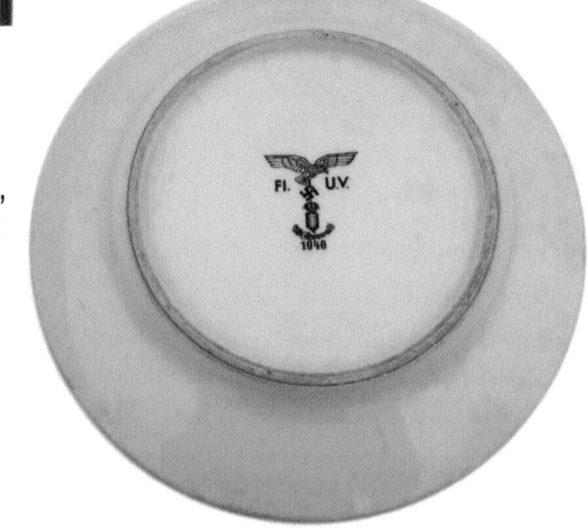


WW II Luftwaffe inert incendiary bomb. Standard Luftwaffe 1 kg bomb. The fins and body retain virtually all of the original paint, clear markings and 1936 date. Ideal for any Battle of Britain or Blitz period display.
**SOLD for**
**$220 / £145 / €203**

Original 1939 framed watercolour of the Hindenburg. An impressive and highly detailed watercolour painted in 1939 by J. HAMWORTHY. Research shows Hamworthy was a serving Royal Engineers Officer, seconded to the RAF and later to become a cartoonist. Measuring 620x260 mm (32"x 26") the attention to detail is excellent. Hamworthy has added a period German biplane to his work to emphasize the scale.

**SOLD for**
**$560 / £360 / €503**

WW I Italian Air Force silver tray / wine coaster. 140 mm in diameter and dated 1937. Captured by British troops in 1941 and marked with crude punched wording Dire Daua 1941, the airfield from which it was liberated.

**SOLD for**
**$187 / £120 / €167**

For more information about current sales, or to share your own buying and selling experiences and receive regular updates on current collecting trends, visit WWW.TRENDINGCOLLECTIBLES.COM

Lightning Source UK Ltd.
Milton Keynes UK
UKIC01n0029060615
253005UK00001B/1

* 9 7 8 1 9 4 3 4 9 2 0 0 8 *